DICK FEHNEL
LESSONS FROM GRAVERS SCHOOL

Memoirs

of

Richard A. Fehnel

First published in 2007 by the Centre for Higher Education Transformation,
House Vincent, 10 Brodie Road, Wynberg Mews, Wynberg, South Africa
www.chet.org.za

Published in paperback in 2009

978-1-920355-04-3

© 2007 Richard A. Fehnel

Edited by Fathima Dada
Designed and typeset by COMPRESS.dsl www.compressdsl.com
Printed by Lightning Source

Contents

Preface iv
Foreword vii

Chapter 1   In the Beginning 1
Chapter 2   Gravers School 9
Chapter 3   The Farm 21
Chapter 4   "Eats" 29
Chapter 5   Free to Roam 39
Chapter 6   The Family Implodes 45
Chapter 7   A New Beginning 57
Chapter 8   *Semper Fidelis* 77
Chapter 9   Cancer Round One 89
Chapter 10   An Intellectual Awakening 101
Chapter 11   Academe 115
Chapter 12   External Consulting and Inner Conflict (1983–1991) 133
Chapter 13   The South African Years (1991–2000) 143

Postscript 167

Bibliography 170

Preface

Dick was involved at the very beginning with the "idea of CHET" (the Centre for Higher Education Transformation) as well as with its formation. But Dick was more than just a "founding funder". The transformation of South African higher education became his *raison d'être* in the last stage of his career. He loved participating in the debates and seminars that CHET organized and was always responsive to funding requests for urgent transformation issues pertaining to the emerging new system. So, the CHET Board had no hesitation in responding positively to the idea of assisting, through its access to editorial and publication expertise, with the publication of Dick's memoirs.

Dick did not leave himself enough time to finish the last project of his career (perhaps an unintended lesson for us). During the period leading up to his "ultimate deadline" (two to four weeks according to his doctor), Dick dictated his thoughts while Dorene transcribed, completing a full circle from the start of their courtship, when she used to type his term papers.

The lack of time deprived Dick of one of his favorite activities— reflections leading to lessons. We thought that it would be helpful, particularly to people who did not know Dick well, if we identified a number of themes or threads that we believe are woven into the narrative. Each of these themes has a certain tension, or contradiction, with which Dick grappled during the journey of his life.

Theory and practice
From practical, commonsense farm-hand education and lessons to abstract academia, and from making community service an integral part of degree programs to making consultancy work practical, Dick engages throughout his career with the elusive links, and lack of links, between principles and practices.

Innovating and doing
From Dick's first job in military training, where he was intrigued by new wartime uses for helicopters, to his last innovation in South African higher education, new and innovative ways of doing things always excited him. But, despite his strong commitment to linking theory to practice, Dick repeatedly describes his ongoing struggle with the "boredom of implementation" and the drudgery of teaching the same class more than once. At one point he rather reluctantly concedes that "the chase was the source of my enthusiasm".

Direct and indirect reform
This dilemma threads through Dick's higher education career. From instigating both curriculum and political reform within the universities where he worked, to supporting transformation projects through USAID and the Ford Foundation, Dick was an incorrigible reformer. But his actual reforming role changed from being directly involved in his own workplace in his own country, to becoming an "invisible hand" in a number of developing countries. For Dick the latter role was very ambiguous. Despite describing himself as a "partner in change" with NGOs, he found it very difficult not to be part of "the power of learning by doing", thus embodying the perennial tension of being a funder of reform. Perhaps this was the root of his preoccupation with "lessons".

Connectedness and disconnectedness
This theme starts with the idyllic Pennsylvania rural life, particularly the individualized, rooted moral education, which taught him lessons that he applied throughout his life. But even in paradise there was disconnectedness. The early loss of a mother and the arrival of a "step mother from hell" started a life-long sequence of disconnecting and then reaching out to reconnect—such as the time

he got tears in his eyes after Professor Ndebele asked him to join the South Africans in the US customs queue at Kennedy airport.

The private and the public
All memoirs face the inevitable dilemma of how much private life to make public. But for Dick this was also an issue in his professional life, and although he became quite intimate friends with some of his professional colleagues, large parts of his life remained private—such as his life in Pennsylvania, his illness, and the anguish he felt about being the "educator analyser who could not help his children". It also raises the familiar question about artists, who dream about connectedness and wholeness, but are often at their best when somewhat dislocated and on the edge.

Nico Cloete and Fathima Dada
September 2007

Foreword

I'm sitting here, looking at the computer screen, wondering if I have the courage to start this project. I'm in my sixty-seventh year, staring death by cancer in the face … again; I'm undergoing chemotherapy and experiencing the usual fatigue and depression associated with this treatment. My wife and others have been after me for years to write about my life, given the odd twists and turns it has taken and the challenges faced and overcome, all against a backdrop of humble beginnings.

Besides giving in to their exhortations, I'm searching for a deeper reason to setting out on this expedition down memory lane. But maybe I shouldn't look for a deeper meaning; maybe I should just write about things as they happened, or as I remember them, and let others look for the deeper meanings.

I would like these stories to have some special meaning to my nineteen-year-old granddaughter, Dara, and two-year-old grandson, Wyatt, neither of whom is likely to help a calf being born; or watch a meadow turn blue as the spring sun calls forth the wild bluebells; or smell the hot, humid, pungent odors of a barn full of cattle when you first open the door on a bitterly cold winter morning; or experience what it's like to answer nature's call in an outhouse, when the wooden seat is covered in a thick layer of frost, and snow is seeping through the cracks in the door; or witness the formal and informal processes of learning in a one-room country schoolhouse, with one teacher and eight grades of learners, huddled around a pot-bellied coal stove on a cold winter day (in the time when "snow days" weren't heard of) sharing desks, books, and the secrets of life that transcend the prescribed curriculum in ways which reveal life's mysteries with a reality that stays with you the rest of your life. These experiences have shaped what I am, for good or for bad. Knowing them is essential to really knowing me.

To those of us born before World War II, the turn of the 21st century seems to portend the loss of a way of life that made America great, ushering in forces that may lead America down the paths of England, Spain, Holland, and skipping a few centuries, Rome, Greece and Persia—paths of declining economic, military and moral power. The sense of loss I refer to is, on one level, confoundingly complex, but on another, confoundingly simple. What follows refers, often indirectly and implicitly, to those losses that seemed at the time not so much as losses as things that were discarded because newer and better things had come along; or so it seemed.

This is a story of a life in transition: from rural beginnings, when electricity was just coming to America's farmlands, to life in urban America, where the escalating division between wealth and poverty is masked by the collusion of corporate greed, media incompetence and a political wasteland. Mother Nature, through the force of Hurricane Katrina, may have revealed these illusions, but I suspect that the strength of humanity's commitment to the Seven Deadly Sins will prevent us from correcting the wrongs of men or the whims of Nature. Oh dear, there I go sounding more and more like Oppenheimer, Heilbronner and Humphrey.* Let's get back to my story.

It is a story, like many of my generation, of "firsts": the first male in my family to go off to college and finish with a Ph.D.; the first generation when most sons did not follow the careers of their fathers, and most daughters, unlike their mothers, began careers other than as housewives. It is also the generation of so many "lasts": the last generation whose educational achievements and economic

---

* J. Robert Oppenheimer, Robert Heilbronner and Hubert Humphrey were three 20th century Americans, distinguished leaders in the fields of science, economics and politics. Their optimistic embrace of life led them to prominence, but in the end all three became pessimistic at best, cynical at worst, about human nature.

accomplishments were greater than the previous generation, thereby ending a run of steady progress that had lasted many generations and defined America as *the* land of opportunity in an otherwise world of rigid caste and class barriers. We were the last generation to know from first-hand experience where our daily food came from, and what our fathers and mothers actually did on a day-to-day basis because we watched them do it. And most of my generation went to church regularly before we came of age.

It is also a generation of simultaneous firsts and lasts—perhaps more so than any other generation in history—demonstrating the increasingly rapid pace of change in our lives, and thereby suggesting some root causes of societal and national angst, anomie and decline. Mine was the first and last generation to actually dial a telephone, and to have our imagination shaped by radio. It was the first and last generation to use a mimeograph machine as the primary means of duplicating documents, and the first and last generation to depend on carbon paper for copies when the mimeo wouldn't do. We were the first and last generation to use electric typewriters on a wide scale in the home and on the job. If you're in this generation, you can probably think of other pairs of firsts and lasts.

This is not the time or place to start an argument about the validity of the sentiment as to whether we, individually and collectively, as a society and a nation, are better or worse off now than we were, say, forty years ago. So, let me just tell this story, and after reflection you may wish to judge for yourself the value of this tale: whether my experiences, which were undoubtedly shared by millions of my generation, helped point us in the direction we are headed today, and whether we are inexorably headed towards decay and decline.

Family photo *circa* 1941.
(From left to right) Harold, Lina, Robert (back), Richard (front), Eula Fehnel.

Chapter 1
In the Beginning

SEPTEMBER 26 WAS A GLORIOUS AUTUMN DAY, DECEIVING US ALL INTO BELIEVING THAT THE DARK DAYS OF THE DEPRESSION MIGHT BE BEHIND US AND THE FUTURE MIGHT BE BRIGHTER AND HAPPIER THAN THE LAST DECADE.

I was born on the first day of the potato-picking season in 1938. Since my father was a potato farmer, I think this was a pretty auspicious beginning. I'd also like to think that it was a classic autumn day in the Lehigh Valley of Pennsylvania; frost revealed by the first rays of dawn, but quickly turning to dew as the day warmed, except in the shadows of the five huge maple trees that stood on the west side of our hundred-year-old farm house, next to the blacktop road.

I'd also like to think that my father paced just outside the bedroom door on the second floor of the farmhouse. But knowing his sense of priorities, he was probably out in the potato field just to the south of the house, organizing the potato pickers and the other farm hands. After all, I was the third child of Harold and Eula Fehnel, and the second son, so that robbed my moment of any originality, even though I was the first and last Fehnel to be born in that old house.

The first day of potato-picking season was, to a potato farmer—and my father was a future president of the Pennsylvania Potato Growers Association—as important a "birthing" as you can imagine. After months of hilling, weeding and spraying, it was the day you found out how good or bad the crop would be. Would it be twenty or a hundred bushels to the acre? Would the potatoes be disease free and good-sized, meaning they could be bagged in fifteen-pound bags and sold directly to consumers at the local A&P for top dollar, or would they be mangy-looking, or diseased, like the apples in our ill-tended orchard, which were used mainly for making apple sauce and cider and feeding the pigs. Since potatoes were our cash crop at that time (before we added the dairy), these differences were really important. They meant whether we would put small change or crisp bills in the church collection plate; they meant whether we would get any presents at Christmas; whether we would get new shoes that year—not that that was going to be a concern for me in 1938.

So that day was important to my dad, and I'm sure he was out in the field, but occasionally looking up at the second story of the south side of the house, at the last window on the left, to see if Dr Brong was signaling whether it was another hand for barn chores or for kitchen chores. I'm sure that my four-year-old sister, who hovered around outside the bedroom door, knew somehow it was an important day, what with all our mother's Grange friends there to help Dr Brong.

But I doubt whether my eight-year-old brother was pumped up by the prospect of my arrival. He was at nearby Gravers School, and probably the upper-most thing on his mind was learning how to better control the nasty fastball he was throwing at the older boys in the baseball game at recess. He was big for his age, a left-hander, and had a scowl like that of Lefty Gomez, a pitching ace of the World Champion New York Yankees (my brother's favorite team), who was striking fear in the hearts of opposing batters as he glowered at them from the pitching mound; like Randy Johnson does for the Yankees today. After all, it was 1938; the World Series was approaching and baseball, America's pastime, was on the minds of American boys of all ages, including my brother. The Yankees were looking to win the Series for an unprecedented third consecutive year, so I'm convinced he was thinking about them. (They did in fact win that year.)

I'd also like to believe that one of the first sounds I became aware of after pushing my way into this strange world was the steady, soothing drone of that old Oliver Model 80 tractor, pulling the single-row potato digger in the field next to the house. In the years ahead I would come to love that ugly but reliable old tractor. By the time I was six or seven, I was steering it, seated on my father's lap. By the time I was eight, my father would put it in gear, set the speed and I was steering it by myself, while my brother walked in the field alongside the tractor's trailer, throwing bales of hay or emptying baskets of potatoes into it.

My birthday meant I'd finally get to see the source of the strange noises I had been hearing for months, noises that I came to realize were voices in two different languages—English and Pennsylvania Dutch. Yes, September 26 was a pretty important day for me, just as it was for the ten or fifteen potato pickers crawling forward on their knees, gathering potatoes as fast as they could, filling a basket, sticking their numbered tag on it and mentally keeping score of the nickels and dimes they were accumulating. It was their last chance to earn some money before all the crops were in, so their hands flew, snatching the freshly dug potatoes and tossing them into the basket they pulled alongside them or the bag they dragged between their legs. Each picker had their own technique, still somewhat rusty on this first day of the potato-picking season, but before the sun reached its noon zenith, most pickers would find some comfort in the form they had regained—even as their backs and legs ached. Old Andrew, the Russian who lived alone in a crude shack at the base of the Blue Mountain, was always the fastest picker, even though he was the oldest by far. When he bent over to start picking in a row of freshly dug potatoes, he wouldn't stand up again until he reached the end of the row. He was amazing.

A few years later my sister and I would ride with my father as he drove around the community picking up those who could come to pick potatoes. We would have to sit on someone's lap as they squeezed into the truck. That routine ended when migrant workers from the South, following the crops northward, became our main source of potato pickers.

September 26 was a glorious autumn day, deceiving us all into believing that the dark days of the Depression might be behind us and the future might be brighter and happier than the last decade. But in the fall of 1938, Lehigh Valley farmers didn't have time to monitor the news closely. The storm clouds they worried about were the ones that billowed over the rolling Pennsylvania hills to the west, not the ones gathering over Europe. They worried about getting the corn in, getting the potatoes in, squeezing one more hay cutting in … anything that would help to put a little more money in the bank to pay for next spring's fertilizer and seeds and to start the annual gamble all over again.

Little did my honest, hard-working father realize that in just over three years our country would be plunged into another world war; that some of the young men picking potatoes or driving tractors in the fields of our farm would die in foreign fields and never again feel the excitement of the first day of potato-picking season.

My first recollections of the war period included the blackouts. We would cover all our windows at night so no light could escape and guide enemy bombers to the nearby Bethlehem Steel Company. I also vaguely remember that my father worked in the steel company during the winter months when farm life was least demanding. I remember the family drama when my aunt's fiancee, a tail gunner in a B-17, was shot down over France and declared Missing in Action.

He was later found alive and well protected by French farmers until he could get back to US lines. I remember when Uncle Harry and Aunt Meda's son was killed on the beach at Anzio, Italy, in 1944—the only Fehnel to die serving his country in that war.

But mostly I remember the quiet playtime I enjoyed in the summers, in the shade of the maple trees. There was an irregular patch of lawn between the sidewalk and the fence that divided our yard from the blacktop road that ran next to our house and barn. This island of grass never grew very much because of the shade from the maple trees. Crisscrossed by veins of dirt, it became my primary playground as a toddler. It was here that my imagination found a daily challenge on the hot summer days. The dirt veins became roads over which my toy cars and trucks moved, propelled by my hands and the motor-like sounds little boys can make almost from the day they are born. Depressions in the grass, where tree roots curled around, became garages or barns where the cars and trucks were carefully parked overnight, and in the morning I would run outside, the screen door slamming behind me, to make sure that they were still where I had left them. Sometimes my sister joined me in this magical place. On other days she played on the other side of the house between the kitchen and the wash-house, making mud pies and sticking flower petals on them while they baked in the sun.

The hot, humid summer days brought the inevitable late afternoon thunderstorm, and often the whole family would sit on the front porch to enjoy the show. Well, at least the kids enjoyed these events; my father would worry about the damage the storms could cause. And he was right to worry. Lightning strikes could start a barn on fire or kill cattle; winds could blow down huge swaths of grain fields before they could be harvested; heavy rains could open big gashes across fields, or beat an alfalfa field or a wheat field into submission, ruining it in a matter of minutes. But to us kids, the summer thunderstorms meant a shallow pool of rainwater was quickly created in front of the porch, and we would cavort barefooted and shirtless in it, splashing away the layers of sweat that had built up during the day in the pre-storm press of heat and humidity.

Summers were also the time of picnics—not just a picnic for our family, but social events that brought together many of the farm families in Moore Township. These were very special occasions that lasted well into the evening, and were made possible by the farm men and all the older boys teaming up to do the chores quickly at one farm after another, just like the team efforts at barn-raising made famous by the Amish (but practiced in all farm communities). These picnics were usually events of the Grange, a social institution in rural America that has essentially disappeared. There was a special picnic ground next to a wooded area, which had a bandstand, outdoor toilets and a building that was transformed into a big booth where soda pop, penny candy and hot dogs were sold. The building also had basic kitchen facilities, which the women could use to heat meals and wash dishes.

Farm women would work for days preparing the "eats", which were shared potluck-style on tables laden with Pennsylvania Dutch summer dishes. The younger men and boys inevitably organized a softball game; the older men pitched horseshoes or quoits; the younger boys and girls played hide-and-go-seek and countless other games around the parked cars and in the adjoining woods.

The highlight of the evening was the "cake walk". Creative farm wives made fabulous cakes, and the cakes were proudly displayed on a table in the center of the bandstand, usually guarded by a bevy of giggling teenage girls. Tickets to enter a circle around the bandstand were sold and, when the circle was full, the master of ceremonies would hold up one cake that was to be the prize on the next "walk". Then he started the people in the circle walking in one direction while he spun a big pointer—a weather vane, as I seem to recall—in the opposite direction. Before the pointer stopped spinning the walkers would be bought to a halt, and everyone seemed to lean in the direction of the needle as it slowly came to a stop. The MC would then sight along the needle and whomever it was pointing at would be the winner of the cake, accompanied by groans from the unlucky ticket holders standing nearby. If I remember correctly, the custom was that no one started eating their cakewalk prize until all the cakes had been claimed. Big families had an advantage over small families, as each member of the family would buy a ticket and the family would try to occupy as lengthy a segment of the circle as they could—usually to the friendly jeering of others—to increase their chances of winning more than one cake. Sometimes, if they won two cakes, the MC would banish them from the circle, to the great delight of the remaining ticket holders.

After gorging ourselves on cake and ice-cream, everyone would pitch in and help clean up the park, and then we would settle down in the backseat for the ride home, exhausted from the day's activities, our minds replaying and remembering the fun of playing with other kids. I don't think I ever made it home from one of these picnics without falling asleep in the big back seat of our old Oldsmobile, even though it was no more than a twenty-minute ride.

For a farm kid, whose only playmate might be a sibling (if they were too young to be doing chores), these occasions were very special. They provided an opportunity to play with other kids all afternoon and evening, generally without supervision. Remember, 1938 was a time before pre-school or kindergarten—at least in Moore Township—even before television, and so the chances for kids and their parents to socialize with other families were looked forward to and enjoyed by all.

There was an interesting documentary on public television recently about the annual Grange Fair in Centre County of Pennsylvania, not too far from Northampton County where I grew up. Centre County's Grange Fair was unique. It had dedicated space for the family tents provided by the organizers for the week of the fair. Once a family got on the tent list, they held onto it for generations, so powerful was the need, the desire, to be close to others and to share the joys and trials of living in rural and small-town America. Our family, and the other families of Moore Township had the Grange Fair, the Church, the social organizations like the Odd Fellows (for the men folk) and the Order of the Eastern Star (for the women) to meet their social needs. As for kids, the one-room country school was our center of life and learning during most of the year. Sundays meant Sunday School, but that didn't really provide much opportunity for fun and games, so we really looked forward to summer picnics.

Gravers School, First Grade class, May 1945.
Dick, 1st grade, front row, third from right. Lina (sister), 5th grade, back row, second from right. The "dreaded" Rev. Dr Klauss presiding.

Chapter 2
Gravers School

THERE IS NO BETTER WAY TO SEE IF YOU REALLY KNOW
A TOPIC THAN TO TRY TO TEACH IT TO SOMEONE
WHO IS HAVING TROUBLE WITH IT.

The sizzle of snow-encrusted mittens hitting the heat shield around the pot-bellied stove in the middle of the one-room school is a sound I remember fondly. It meant we had a great time at recess or lunch, building crude snow forts and having pitched snowball battles.

The smell of hot, wet woolen mittens drying was soon accompanied by the smell of baking potatoes. Kids would bring a raw potato for lunch, with their initials or some other identifying mark carved into the skin. After recess, when the coals were banked into a mantle of ash-encrusted embers, the teacher would gently put our potatoes on the coals, and by lunch-time the smell of baked potatoes permeated the classroom. Some kids would bring home-made soup, and heat it on the top of the stove, while others would heat their bologna-and-cheese sandwiches on the stove-top.

I cannot describe with sufficient precision and emotion the depth of appreciation I have for the learning—formal and informal—that I acquired in that old schoolhouse. One teacher and about 30 kids, ranging over eight grades. The younger kids sat in the small desks (two to a desk) near the front of the classroom; the older kids sat in the larger desks at the back of the classroom. Four double hung windows on opposing walls provided the light for learning. A blackboard spanned the width of the classroom behind the teacher's desk, which sat on a platform one step above the classroom floor. At the back two doors led into the narrow cloakroom that ran the width of the building. In the middle of the outside wall one door, framed by a window on either side, was our proverbial door to learning.

The floor of the entire building was oak, and at the start of every school year it was daubed with a protective coat of a preservative that gave it a dark sheen and a distinct petroleum-like odor that I can still smell. On the wall above the blackboard, behind the teacher's desk, Washington and Lincoln monitored our learning and our behavior. On good days, they had faint, benign smiles. On bad days, I swear you could see Washington pursing his lips, and his eyes turning steely gray in disapproval, while Lincoln just looked a little sadder. Beneath these pictures the upper edge of the blackboard held a border consisting of the letters of the alphabet, in cursive and block, capital and lower case script. Off to the teacher's right, against the wall, was a storage cabinet that held all our tools of learning: books on the bottom shelf and paper, pencils, glue, scissors and other supplies on the upper one. To the left of the teacher, against the opposite wall, a United States flag, to which we pledged allegiance every morning (without controversy), stood guard over a map of the world and a map of the USA. Next to the maps, facing into the corner, was a solitary chair—the destination of any child whose behavior got out of hand. When the Rev. Dr Klauss was the teacher, in my first grade, he conspicuously hung on a row of pegs next to the chair his collection of wire belts that he used for administering corporal punishment—an earlier version of shock and awe. Since he was about six foot two and quite husky, he seldom used the belts, but when he did, the victim had generally pissed in his pants before the first blow landed.

Now that image certainly doesn't sound like "the good old days", unless, of course, you still live in a cave and beat your kids regularly. But it is a small part of the collage of memories that flood my mind when I think of my days at Gravers School. The much greater part of the mental collage is made up of images of the incredible dynamics of learning in that simple classroom. Embedded in the daily processes of learning were valuable principles that have stood the test of time, and which I was to use when I became a teacher.

There is an old Chinese proverb that goes "I hear and I forget, I see and I remember, I do and I understand". I had that printed in bold letters and hung prominently in my office when I was a professor at the University of Oregon. I learned the wisdom of that proverb in Gravers School. The teacher for five of the six years I attended Gravers School was Mrs Bossard. She never lectured for 45 minutes to any of the classes. Rather, she would call the students in a given grade to the front of the classroom, where they sat in the seats immediately in front of the first and second graders. She would ask questions about the assignment and they would answer—sort of following the Socratic technique. Her method included making frequent use of the big blackboard, both by her and by the students. And, in the language of today, she regularly empowered students to undertake a variety of experiments, usually to do with the physical world. The broad window sills of the school were shoulders that supported terrariums, aquariums, and exotic flora and fauna.

So, any learner sitting in that classroom could hear, see and witness the doings of the other learners. And that open learning environment made it possible for the fast learners to listen in on what the kids in a grade or two ahead of them were learning, and to begin thinking about those things. And, for the slower learners, it was possible to listen in on stuff they were still having trouble with as she introduced it to the lower grades. This was a concrete application of the principle of redundancy, which is so valuable to most learners, but which seems to have been lost in today's crowded curricula. And if you were still having problems, she made sure that you received one-on-one tutoring from one of the older students. There is no better way to see if you really know a topic than to try to teach it to someone who is having trouble with it.

To be totally honest, not all of us who periodically sat with an older tutor were actually motivated by a desire to learn. I can't remember her name, or even what she looked like, but I can remember the mildly intoxicating scent of the sixth grade girl who occasionally tutored me—not that I actually needed it. I can also remember the softness of her skin when our arms brushed against each other. It was always the older girls who were given the responsibility of tutoring. With good reason—most of the older boys had little interest in nurturing anything other than their own emerging masculinity.

The daily routine of the school had a definite structure, but it was subtle and flexible. There were no bells, no sudden rush of students from the classroom into jammed hallways, no slamming of locker doors or chirping of cell phones. The flow of one grade of students to the front of the classroom was as gentle as the flow of a spring brook, and accompanied by as mellow a murmur as one would have heard sitting on the brook's bank. I know because I spent hours by such a brook, just as I spent hours listening and watching the flow of learners to and from the front of the classroom. Mrs Bossard was firm, but friendly; empathetic but not a push-over. She managed that school in a manner that I, a so-called expert in management with a Ph.D., still find a mystery and a wonder.

Many years later, when I was teaching at the University of Oregon, I was bemused by the development of a so-called innovative and experimental "school within a school" in the neighborhood elementary school our son was attending. It attempted to recreate the environment that had nurtured my thirst for learning by putting learners from four grades (not eight) together with four (not one) teacher, in four (not one) classroom. It was chaos. They gave it up after a few years. They tried too many things at once—too much democracy, too much "learner autonomy", too much parent involvement, and too little focus on the actual learning of reading, writing and arithmetic. The basic problem was that none of those who espoused this "new" approach to learning had ever been schooled in a real one-room school, with one teacher and eight grades. Their efforts were guided by theory, and not informed by experience.

Experience is the master teacher in our lives. "I do and I understand" ... especially if I screw up. In Gravers School we experienced through the older students—directly or vicariously—many of the lessons of life, and what we didn't experience there, in that one-room schoolhouse or the playground that surrounded it, we experienced on the farms where we lived. We didn't need a sex-education class, we saw the mechanics of procreation regularly on our farms. And the older kids made sure we understood how it worked with people, because they had been told by their older siblings or cousins. Our physics lab was the great rope strung between two trees on the playground. A couple of the bigger kids began swinging this rope, like a giant jump rope, while other kids jumped into the arc, and grabbed the rope as it flew past. If they were lucky they were able to wrap their arms and legs around the rope and hang on for dear life. The physics part of this entertainment was to see who would fly the farthest and bounce the highest when they let go. Another physics experiment entailed a large stone and an oak plank. Together they created a lever with a fulcrum, just like the illustration in the physics book. One day at lunch-time, with that lever, we raised the back wheels of Mrs Bossard's car just a quarter inch off the ground, while a brave kid put bricks under the axle.

Our psychology lab was comparing the differences between Rev. Dr Klauss as a teacher and as a person (a bachelor who literally lived in his car, having removed the back seat so he could put a stove in there, with a hole cut through the roof for the chimney) and Mrs Bossard as a teacher and as a person. Most interesting was how they responded to that wonderful but long lost tradition of "Lock Out Day".

Lock Out Day was the day before the start of Lent. I have no idea when the tradition began, or even why it was celebrated, but it was an event that students looked forward to each year, as one looked forward to April Fool's Day or Halloween, back in the days when Halloween meant playing pranks, such as tipping over the neighbor's outhouse.

On Lock Out Day some of the students would try to get to the school before the teacher arrived. If they were lucky, the window they had surreptitiously left unlocked the day before was still unlocked, and they would clamber through and secure the school's only door from the inside, so the teacher couldn't open it. By the time the teacher arrived, most of the kids would be there, either inside with the perpetrators or gathered outside waiting to see how the charade played out. The teacher would make a great scene trying to get in, then give up disgustedly, declare the day a holiday, and all would go home happy—even the teacher.

But, Lock Out Day with Rev. Dr Klauss was something else! He turned crimson; the veins in his thick neck throbbed. He shouted threats at the top of his voice, in English and Pennsylvania Dutch, so there couldn't be any doubt about what he was saying. I don't remember the details of how he got in, but he did, and school began … with beatings for the ring leaders. There could be no doubt that he saw Lock Out as a direct challenge to his supreme authority, and he clearly relished the opportunity to demonstrate his authority through his wire belts. I remember the smaller children whimpering in the front desks, a few cried openly even though it was the older boys getting the whipping. Not that spankings were rare in those days. Most children experienced them from their parents—the days of "Spare the Rod and Spoil the Child". This was 1944 (when I was in first grade) and it was two years before Dr Benjamin Spock published his book that froze the hands with the rods.

So, Lock Out Day was a disaster … for the kids. I suspect that Rev. Dr Klauss was secretly keeping score, that he had never been successfully locked out, and that he had notched up quite a few beatings in the process.

Lock Out Day with Mrs Bossard was another matter entirely, thus my claim that comparing the two teachers was our psych lab. Mrs Bossard drove up in her 1940 black Chevy sedan (no stove pipe in her car roof), feigning surprise at seeing all the kids already there, since she usually arrived well before the kids began arriving. She gathered her things and headed for the door, followed by kids barely able to contain their giggles—except for the second graders, who probably still had nightmares from last year's events thanks to the Rev. Dr Klauss. Finding the door couldn't be opened after she had unlocked it, she pretended that she couldn't understand what was wrong with the lock, and continued to fuss about some mysterious mechanical problem. At that point, little Georgie Wambold couldn't contain himself any longer and shrieked, in perfect Pennsylvania Dutch, "It's Lock Out Day, Teacher!" He was so excited, he couldn't stand still, and I thought he was going to wet his pants.

"Oh, dear," feigned Mrs Bossard. "What can we do?" And then with a twinkle in her eye she headed back to her car, but instead of getting in the front seat and driving off, according to some scripts, she opened the trunk. There, in perfect order, were several dozen of her homemade doughnuts—the prescribed morning food for Shrove Tuesday. She handed them out with great ceremony, lifting each one and waving it to the boys whose hungry faces were pressed against the windows on the inside of the locked school before putting it in the eager hands stretched out to her. When she was down to her last box, she held them up to the boys in the window and beckoned them out with a wiggle of an index finger. Soon the front door opened and a half dozen or so of the bigger boys sheepishly came out, eager to collect the Lock Out Day doughnuts she had made for us. After we had eaten them all, school began as usual.

Psych Lab 101 had ended for the day, for those making the comparison between Mrs Bossard and the Rev. Dr Klauss.

Not all of our learning was confined to the classroom or playground. Walking the half mile to school each day provided its own learning opportunities. I usually walked with the three Wetzel kids (Bobby, Irene and Gizella), the two Haftls (Shirley and Donald), Joey Nemchik, and for several years, my sister, Lina. We learned to debate (which was better, John Deere or Oliver tractors; which breed of cattle was better for milk, Holsteins or Guernseys; who were smarter, girls or boys?) We learned which flowers bloomed first in the spring; on which side of the road the snow was likely to be highest and last longer and why; what the differences were between Catholic and Lutheran Orders of Service. We argued about politics, religion, sports—the same things our parents would have argued about if rural conventions of good behavior could be dropped for a moment. We took home the points made by the others, and got our parents views—if they had one—on how to counter an argument. We learned when to drop an argument, intuitively finding that space where friendship trumped winning. It takes a long time to walk half a mile when you're a kid, and it could be pretty lonely walking by yourself, so you learned discretion about many things, just as our parents did.

Most of the time the walk to and from school was uneventful. Gravers School was a half mile north of our farmhouse, along side the black ribbon of macadam that ran south from the village of Crossroads, where my paternal grandparents had a country store, to where it joined the concrete highway that ran from Bath, Pennsylvania, up to the Blue Ridge mountains, the southern-most rib of the Appalachians that marked our northern horizon. But in the winter, when wind and snow whipped across the stubble of the cornfield and stung our faces and hands as it tried to find unprotected flesh, around a collar or up a sleeve, that half-mile became a challenge. We would huddle together, the bigger kids in the front, taking the brunt of the wind; the smaller kids in the back, leaning forward and looking for a just-vacated footprint in the deepening snow to put their own tiny boots.

Ours was the last inhabited farm before the school, so the Wetzels, Haftls and Joey Nemchik, who had already walked about half a mile, would stop in our farm kitchen to savor a last minute flush of warmth from our big coal stove. Then we would head out, dutifully walking on the left side of the narrow macadam road that went straight as an arrow northward past our farm until it reached Crossroads. Our first steps were up the slight hill next to our barn, where the snowdrifts were the deepest, then across the 300 yards of the "plain of Abraham", the flat fields north of our barn that were our farm's highest point and were bisected by the macadam road, down the hill and across a dry stream-bed, up a slight gradient and just a shiver of a twist in the macadam as it passed between the abandoned house and barn of the farm next to ours and then straight again for the last 250 yards to the school ground, on the east side of the road, next to the dirt road that intersected with our macadam ribbon. In that last stretch of road, from the abandoned farm to the school, the field on the east side of the road was about four feet higher than the road bed, which meant snow drifts in winter, so we usually walked that section in the field above the road.

Making that daily trip taught us diligence. We learned that we were capable of making that walk regardless of the weather, regardless of how miserable we felt. We learned the value of doing tough things in good company. When someone felt poorly, they could count on someone else carrying their school bag. On *really* nasty days, we would pile in the back of the pickup and our hired hand, Clinty Graver, would drive us the last half-mile. And more than once when snowdrifts made the road impassable, I remember my father hitching a wagon to a tractor and taking us in it across the fields to school.

Recess time was also a time of learning—of how to deal with the bigger kids. They usually organized the games and made sure everyone played fair. In the winter there were pitched snowball battles; in the fall and spring there were games of football, baseball, fox and geese, and "Red Rover, Red Rover", with kids of all ages playing together. We had learned at home to play with siblings of different ages, and this carried over naturally to the playground at Gravers School. And in this way we were spared the age stratification our city cousins endured, a process that puts off learning how to deal with others older or younger than yourself. While there were no bullies at Gravers there were the occasional fights, but you learned to sort things out among yourselves. The age-based cliques so common in suburban schools of today didn't exist, nor did gangs as we know them today in the ghettos and *barrios* of our cities. Consequently, the fierce peer pressures that contort the development of today's youth didn't exist, at least not to the same degree it seems to today. Play time and study time at Gravers operated, in terms of social dynamics, on a principle of centrifugal force. Because of the small numbers in each age group (for example, my brother was the only one in his grade for a number of years) and the close interaction we had with each other all day long, we were forced "outward" and learned across a range of skills and behaviors. In contrast, today's schools, with their large age-specific classes, act on a principle of centripetal social force, with interactions more intense within a limited range. And in that intense crucible of social dynamics, much of it without adult supervision, the opportunities to learn a range of ways to deal with those older and younger than you are put off, and in some cases it seems, never really learned at all.

Later, when I was in seventh grade, the school district began a consolidating process, and rather than finishing seventh and eighth grade at Gravers, I was bussed to junior high school in the nearby town of Bath (population of 1500, more or less). The consolidating plan eventually deepened to include all grades, and Gravers School sat empty for several years. I felt really sad every time I passed it; it had meant so much to me. Finally, the school district sold it and someone converted it into a home, which it still is. For years the conversion did not change the physical exterior of the building; the steeple with the bell was still there, and the building looked happy as little feet raced around its playground (now a carefully tended yard and garden) and through its door of learning.

But while it was still Gravers School its influence on our lives was substantial. It provided the space where lessons were learned that would be carried through life, where friendships were deepened, and most importantly for many kids, where their roots to Northampton County and the rural life of a farm community were set deep in the soil of their souls. The other day I was trying to recall how many of the twenty-odd kids with whom I shared the Gravers School experience went on to college and left the area. I know the Wedde boys are still there operating the family farm and an auto repair shop, and living on the piece of land where my father dreamed of building his retirement house. Joe Nemchik went off to college in Indiana, but came back to Pennsylvania to work and, now retired, lives just a few miles away from Gravers School. Bobby Wetzel still lives on the family homestead, and probably drives past the school several times a week. The Kochers and Itterlys, the first "blended family" of my generation, still lived within sight of the school several years ago when I last visited the area. Relatively few of the kids I went to Gravers with went on to high school—at least, their faces do not grace the annual yearbooks of Northampton High School.

My own story took some twists and turns, and instead of graduating from Northampton High, I graduated from Allentown High School in 1956, then the largest public high school in the state of Pennsylvania. I'll be relating these twists and turns later, but for the moment I want to wander around the memories of Gravers School and the farm years.

1948.
Dick and the 4-H Blue Ribbon calf he raised.

Chapter 3
The Farm

"DO IT ONCE, DO IT RIGHT, GET IT DONE."
I MUST HAVE HEARD THOSE WORDS A THOUSAND
TIMES FROM MY FATHER OR CLINTON GRAVER,
OUR MAIN FARM-HAND.

Suddenly the door opened wide at the top of the steep steps leading down into the cool cellar, where the four of us were sitting on the damp slate floor. We had left the door open slightly so that a little sunlight would find its way down to where we were, at the bottom of the cool cellar.

I should explain for those unfamiliar with a cool cellar that it is a space about ten feet underground, accessed by steep steps behind a closed and sometimes locked door. In the days before electricity, every farm had a cool cellar, or a spring house, where food was kept throughout the hot summer. Milk, butter, leftovers, fresh fruit—anything that might spoil or should be served cool was kept there. Something cool, like ... beer.

"Oh, shit!" someone muttered. Someone else coughed, lungs rejecting the sour air of the cigars we were all smoking. The footsteps coming down the steps grew louder.

"Well, well, well!" My father said. I could barely see his face through the cloud of cigar smoke that filled the small space of the cool cellar.

"Cigars AND beer!" my father exclaimed, as he looked at the bottle each of us was clutching. Anger and laughter competed for space on his face. I suppose the sight was really pretty funny, except that the beer was meant for the hired hands at the end of a hard day in hot fields. He had no idea where the nickel cigars came from, and I don't remember either—probably from my grandfather's country store.

"What will you ten-year-olds think of next?"

We were all afraid to hazard an answer.

"Well, since you started them you might as well finish them, so drink up and take a nice deep puff on those cigars." I could detect the irony in my father's voice, and I didn't like where this was headed.

"Mr Fehnel," Bobby Wetzel stammered, "maybe this wasn't a good idea."

"No," my father countered, "it was a very good idea. How else will young boys like you learn that beer and cigars are for men? But you won't learn if you don't finish them. Now take another puff and have another drink."

Time crept by slowly. My father sat on the bottom step, blocking our only exit, silhouetted by the sunlight that was struggling to cut through the deepening blue cloud of smoke from the four cheap cigars. We puffed (and coughed); we drank (and choked). Each of us was trying to nurse a bottle of the best beer in the Lehigh Valley—Neuweillers, from the brewery on Lehigh Street in Allentown—but with each swallow it tasted worse.

"Mr Fehnel," Donnie Haftl moaned, "I don't feel so good."

"What? Already? Why you have half a bottle left, and look how much of that cigar you still have."

Donnie began gagging.

"Oh shit," I thought, "he'll make us clean that up, too."

My dad must have had the same thought, because he stepped down into the cellar with us, opening our stairway to freedom.

"OK you *dumkopfs*, up the stairs!" I could hear him chuckle as he watched us stagger up the stairs and sink to the grass beyond the cool cellar door, blinded by the bright summer sun. We had added shame to the words that described this once brave group of four.

I don't remember if we all threw up, but I do know that none of us ever took up cigar smoking.

Growing up on the farm was such a great place for learning lessons that stayed with you for the rest of your life.

Not all the lessons learned on the farm were about what not to do. Many were lessons about the right things to do—like doing a job correctly the first time, so you only do it once; sticking with a job until it was done, regardless of the boredom or the discomfort it entailed, because starting a disagreeable task a second time puts you in a really bad mood and robs you of the satisfaction of saying, "There, it's done. Now let's go for a swim!"

When the job is mixing a ton or two of the basic elements of feed for the cattle (corn, wheat, molasses, oats, et cetera), scoop by scoop, with one big shovel, you don't want to realize half-way through that you forgot an ingredient, or that you screwed up the amounts. Or if the job is plowing a fifteen-acre field, which can take several days, you don't want to realize that you forgot to set the plow at the correct depth when you're half done. "Do it once, do it right, get it done." I must have heard those words a thousand times from my father or Clinton Graver, our main farm-hand.

I was thinking about some of these lessons the other day, while briskly walking through my forty-minute cardiac rehab routine on the treadmill, when my thoughts were interrupted by the clearly one-sided conversation coming from a guy two machines away. I watched him for a while, out of the corner of my eye. He was wearing a clean, white sweatband, the Nike logo perfectly centered. But he wasn't in danger of sweating. Despite being at least twenty years younger than me, he was trudging along at a mediocre pace. And he was reading his Oregon Mental Health Association Newsletter. And he was, of course, talking on his f**king cell phone; an inane conversation, with no real importance. In the course of the next twenty minutes he made fifteen similar calls, all the while reading his newsletter and walking on the treadmill.

This jerk, who probably was thinking that the others in the gym were admiring his multi-tasking kept looking around as if to see if we were appreciating his abilities when actually he wasn't accomplishing anything. His treadmill pace had no aerobic value; the stuff he was reading he wouldn't be able to remember tomorrow, and the phone calls he made only benefited his cell phone company. They had no real content.

That got me thinking about lessons learned on the farm, and how times have changed. We never thought about multi-tasking, or whatever it might have been called then, because you had to concentrate on doing the one thing you were doing right. The more I think about multi-tasking, the more I am convinced that it breeds mediocrity and allows for a lack of accountability because you never do anything well—just enough to get by and get on to the next task. Multi-tasking allows us to excuse poor performance because we were doing three things at once, none of them extremely well, and everyone who has done three or more things at once will relate to your situation, and let you off the hook.

I think multi-tasking ought to be something that is done very sparingly and only when there really are no alternatives—such as when you are trying to fix breakfast, getting the kids' lunch packed, letting the dog out, and co-ordinating schedules with your spouse.

The reality is that women are much better at multi-tasking than men; they have had to be in order to survive. Most guys think multi-tasking is reading the paper, surfing the channels and pretending to be in a conversation with a spouse or child. Or they think multi-tasking is driving their SUV, talking on the hands-free cell phone, picking their noses and changing radio stations to get last night's scores.

But nowadays multi-tasking has crept into our daily lives to a frightening extent, and worse yet, we treat it as a virtue. We expect our kids to become proficient at this dubious talent, so that they can impress the admissions people at the private kindergarten we want them to attend.

Multi-tasking soaks up free time like a sponge—time that is actually needed for our minds to grow, to imagine and to reflect. The lessons I learned on the farm were generally learned well because there was a lot of time to think about them. We had no TV, no Internet, no gaggle of kids hanging out together. We had chores to do, and after they were done, we read or listened to the radio and let our imaginations soar. We never heard of kids suffering from ADHD in those days. I think it was because kids had time to let their brains work at a pace that was appropriate for healthy mental development. And perhaps the most important thing a mind can do is dream. Without dreams individuals and societies become slaves to whatever entraps them. Johnny Clegg, a South African musician who kept the dream of a day without apartheid alive during the worst of times in the 1980s, writes in one of his songs:

> I saw the Berlin wall fall;
> I saw Mandela walk free;
> I saw a dream whose time has come
> Change my history—so keep on dreaming.
> —Johnny Clegg & Savuka, "Your Time Will Come"

Lord knows I did lots of daydreaming during the days I was growing up on the farm, especially during the "bad years" after my mother died and a madwoman became our stepmother. I dreamed of changing my history; those dreams became a vision, then a plan, then reality. But it was made possible by learning to do things better than anyone else, by setting and maintaining high standards, and having the mental and physical space (we farmed 300 acres) to move around, not tied to the moment by tasks piled on top of each other.

Another valuable lesson I learned on the farm was acceptance of people that were different—no, that's not strong enough—I learned to respect people who were different, and not to judge them. We had two farm hands that were employed full time most of the year. One was Clinton "Clinty" Graver, the same age as my father, a bachelor who had spent time in prison as a conscientious objector and who was a devout Jehovah Witness, and, I suspect, perhaps a latent homosexual. The other was Esther Lily, a lesbian who dressed like a man, had her haircut like a man, and smoked and cursed like a man. I worked side-by-side with them for years; we shared many lunches together; we rode thousands of miles together delivering potatoes or some other product from our farm. They were undoubtedly stigmatized by some in the farming community, but not by our family. Nor did they let the treatment they may have received from others twist the way they interacted with us, or with others. They were two of the hardest working, honest, best natured people I could have grown up with, and many of the perspectives I have about what we call diversity today came from my relationship with them as I grew from toddler to teenager.

Related to the notion of respecting other people, despite their differences from us, was the value of knowing when to keep your opinions to yourself. I can't think of one single incident of seeing my father in an argument with a neighbor or even a stranger. Perhaps he learned that from his father. As I mentioned, my grandfather owned a country store. What I remember of that wonderful place is laughter—never angry words.

But the more I think about it, the more it seems that throughout rural America—and perhaps among rural people worldwide—the value of having peaceful relations with your neighbors was paramount, because you never knew when you might need each other in an emergency. I can remember on more than one occasion leaving the lunch or dinner table hurriedly when a neighbor called to say that he needed help rounding up cattle that had broken out of his pasture. Manpower on a farm is always just enough to keep up with the routines, but never enough to handle emergencies, and if you suddenly need help, you can't easily preface a call for help with an apology for an angry exchange of words. Keeping good relations, I learned, was far more important than being right, no matter how large or small the issue. That doesn't mean being a wimp; it just means that one has to balance what one says and how one says it, with an understanding of the long-range impact it will have on a relationship that may be the difference between weathering an emergency or experiencing a disaster. And so there is this universal convention of behavior among farm folk that says "make nice". Most city folks don't get it, because they don't put their lives at risk every day so much. Farm folk do, and they realize that good relations with their neighbors are the best safety net they can have.

Another lesson I learned on the farm was the simplicity of telling the truth, even when it meant some recrimination. Shakespeare had it right when he observed that we weave tangled webs when we lie, and trying to keep deceitful stories straight just isn't worth the effort. When you are the only one responsible for feeding the chickens and collecting the eggs, or keeping the coal bucket filled and the ashes cleaned out of the kitchen stove, and you forget to do these things, who are you going to blame for your forgetfulness? Just "fess up", take the heat and move on. I couldn't understand why kids would come up with obviously made-up tales about why they hadn't done their homework. The more they lied, the deeper the trouble they created. I think Clinty Graver impressed on me more than anyone else how much easier life would be if we were truthful. I would watch him get angry when I tried to lie my way out of something—angry not at what I had failed to do, but at my lying. His square face, usually sporting a smile, would get hard; his jaw muscles would flex, and his voice would lose its cheerful timbre. His anger never led to a threat, nor any action remotely physical, so I had time to think about what was pushing his buttons, and it didn't take long to realize that not being truthful compounded the damage; better just to admit your shortcoming and make sure it didn't happen again.

In some respects, farm life provided little cover for the events of the day. There wasn't the anonymity provided by the complexity of urban life. But at the same time, that simplicity made it much easier to separate what was important from what was just a diversion.

Learning about life on the farm also had a more structured dimension. When we were older, and in the 4-H Club, the monthly meetings were a time for socializing, as well as learning more about farm life from the County Agent who conducted these meetings. We learned about the diseases that attacked farm animals and crops, and ways to control them; we learned about new farming techniques and equipment, and we learned how young farm kids could become productive members of the farming community. We undertook projects that focused our learning. My brother, sister and I all raised Angus steers and took them to the Allentown Fair for showing. My sister and I also raised sheep as a 4-H Club project, though our father was never really enthusiastic about these dumb animals. We also had garden projects, and sold the garden produce. There were also special projects for girls, like canning and preserving fruit and vegetables, and sewing projects, but my sister was more interested in the projects that boys and girls both participated in.

Learning to stick with these projects to their logical end developed an appreciation of patience. Farm projects adhere to natural life cycles; there is no way you can speed up the raising of a calf to the point where it is producing milk or ready to be sold for slaughter. The same goes for projects that involved crops. So we learned the value of patience instead of the instant gratification our city friends seemed to get from projects that could be completed in just an hour or a day or a weekend.

Chapter 4
"Eats"

EAT YOURSELF FULL.
(PENNSYLVANIA DUTCH SAYING)

One of the pleasures of writing this memoir has been reading up on how others have gone about it. I have gained much from these forays into the written records of the lives of others, from simple things such as chapter headings to more complex challenges of delving into the motivations and methods of people who have had a hand in shaping the lives of others.

Tim Russert's enjoyable and easily readable memoir has one-word chapter headings signaling the values he learned from his father. The chapter headings click along like virtues from a Boy Scout manual: Respect, Work, Faith, Food, Fatherhood. What a clever idea, I thought, to make the topic of food, in a memoir of someone who clearly likes to eat, sound like a virtue that needs to be learned and passed on to younger generations. But when I read his chapter again, it convinced me that in some families the issues of earning the food we put on our tables, how we respect it and respect the process of preparing and consuming it, and use the act of eating as an important opportunity for keeping family together and "on message" as they might say today, is indeed an important lesson.

In the Pennsylvania Dutch culture, which is the bedrock of my soul, "eats" are a very important part of life. I have forgotten many of the tales associated with some of the specific foods, but remember that they had tales that were passed down through generation after generation, and this signaled their value in our culture.

When my bride of Danish, Norwegian, English and German ancestry was introduced to my grandfather, I made sure she knew how to say, "How are you?" in Pennsylvania Dutch. This floored Pappy.

"I didn't know they spoke Pennsylvania Dutch out there in Seattle!" he exclaimed. Dorene and I had just flown from Seattle, boarding the plane straight after our wedding and flying to the East Coast to meet my family for the first time, since none had been able to come to the ceremony.

While Dorene's minimal language preparations may have had some positive initial impact on the family, it didn't prepare her for what lay in store when we sat down to eat this first meal together with my family. To underscore the importance of the occasion, my grandfather made sure the menu included a rare and auspicious Pennsylvania Dutch delicacy—stuffed pig's stomach! To her credit, Dorene gamely tried a small portion, while also eating the more familiar ham and roast beef that was passed around. The meal was a classic Pennsylvania Dutch special dinner; at least three different meat dishes, seven sweets and seven sours, along with at least two kinds of potatoes and enough gravy to clog the arteries of a small army.

Meals like this were an important part of Pennsylvania Dutch life. The few restaurants that specialized in such meals never offered them regularly; they were simply too costly to prepare, and they couldn't charge enough to cover the costs. And if the restaurant tried to cut a few corners (like only two meat dishes and three or four sweet and sour dishes), the word immediately got out and they were either out of business, or they changed the cuisine to something less demanding, more profitable, and where the clientele was less likely to be experts on what was offered and how it was prepared. Maybe that's why Italian and Greek restaurants were popular in the Lehigh Valley.

I grew up on a farm, and my father always said, "We'll eat first, then we'll sell what we don't need." Even when times were tough, in the last days of the Depression and during the war years, there was always fresh food on the table. And every meal started with a prayer, thanking God for the meal we were about to eat and asking a blessing on those who prepared it. Preparing food in those days was much more of a challenge than modern cooks can possibly imagine. Refrigeration was minimal; that's why we had a cool cellar. Heat came from a coal fired stove; there was no running water in the kitchen but there was a hand pump by the sink that drew water from the cistern under the kitchen.

Nevertheless, there were always freshly prepared, delicious meals. In our house they tended to be a combination of Pennsylvania Dutch and Southern dishes, as my mother, whose family had roots in Virginia all the way back to the settling of Jamestown, drew on all her skills to keep us happy. Southern fried chicken, with a side dish of rich gravy and dumplings, was a perfect example of her version of culinary fusion.

Winter each year brought a day of butchering. All other farmwork was set aside this day, and the hired help, as well as my grandparents and one or two family friends with the right skills and knives, also came to help. On this day a steer and several pigs would be slaughtered and their carcasses immediately rendered into many forms of food. The slaughtering took place in the barnyard, and the butchering in the wash-house next to the kitchen. In the wash-house two huge kettles of water were kept hot over coal fires. As the slabs of meat were carried into the wash-house, my father and Uncle Harry sliced the meat into appropriate cuts—steaks, roasts, fillets. Odd pieces were immediately ground for hamburgers and sausages, and everything would be wrapped, marked and hauled down to the homemade freezer in out basement that Dad had made from an old milk cooler from someone's dairy equipment. The cooler could hold about 15 milk cans, so as a freezer it had a generous capacity, and easily held the better part of a butchered steer and two pigs, as well as frozen vegetables and fruit. It also had room to spare for a deer, should the hunting season be successful.

Butchering day was a beehive of activity; the women were kept busy wrapping and marking the meat, as well as immediately cooking some of the offal for tasty snacks, such as crackling—rendered pork fat or skin which is a by-product of making lard. As gross as it may sound to today's youth, it was a real delicacy. The cooked crackling was as crisp as a potato chip and ten times as tasty. Scrapple, another Pennsylvania Dutch breakfast staple, was also made on butchering day. It is a mixture of finely ground pork (the left over bits and pieces), lard, onions and spices that is shaped into a loaf and kept refrigerated until it is sliced and fried, then served with maple syrup or deep-brown apple butter. There was nothing better for breakfast on a cold winter morning than several slices of scrapple to "stick to your ribs" and keep you warm while doing outdoor chores in the cold. As one writer on Pennsylvania Dutch cooking, Lynn Kerrigan, noted, "Scrapple lovers think of it as food for the gods. Anti-scrapplers consider it a culinary abomination."

Butchering day was also the day for salting hams and bacon, wrapping them in brown paper bags and hanging them in the attic for months to cure. For years the smell of curing bacon and hams permeated the attic, whetting the appetite of anyone who had to go looking for anything up there. The aroma never left, even once we had stopped curing ham and bacon. On butchering day my sister and I would rush from school, anxious to get home while there might still be some crackling or some cooked kidneys, sprinkled with salt and pepper, for a very special, once a year after-school snack.

In the spring, when dandelions began sprouting up through the lawn, we learned to pick the most tender leaves so Mom could make a Pennsylvania Dutch springtime staple, dandelion salad with warm bacon dressing. Springtime was also the time for planting the gardens. We had a big garden that took up about one third of our front yard. Here we planted peas, beans, carrots, beets, lettuce—the smaller vegetables that were harvested on a daily basis and served fresh from the garden. A much bigger garden was planted in a triangular piece of land in the field just south of the house. Here the things that took up more space were planted—sweet corn, tomatoes, cucumbers and other things that grew on vines such as watermelons, cantaloupes and various squash and pumpkins. Part of this area was set aside for 4-H Club gardening projects that my sister and I grew, and when the products were ripe we loaded them in the back of our Chevy pickup and peddled them in the suburbs of Bethlehem. There was no sense in putting a farm stall next to the house by the side of the road, as everyone who drove by had their own garden. But taking them to town was a sure way to earn some money and see how city folks lived.

Summers also meant weekends at the family cabin in the nearby Pocono Mountains, where we witnessed the magic of my grandmother's kitchen. Emma Julia Reinhard Fehnel, the daughter of Sylvester Obadiah Reinhard and Sarah Young, was a prototypical Pennsylvania Dutch cook. She could make a feast appear like magic; she never used recipes, always making something wonderful out of the most mundane leftovers. And there was always a pie or cake in the oven. These were skills that Pennsylvania Dutch girls learned—absorbed might be a better way to describe the process—at their mother's side, in the heat of kitchens warmed by wood and coal burning stoves—those wonderful, enamel covered hulks that took up a lot of kitchen space, but were worth every square inch.

Mammy Fehnel, as she was known to all, was able to create a table groaning with food for ten or fifteen people at any time and anywhere, including our summer cabin—a rustic hunting cabin without electricity or running water. There was a small cool cellar under the floor of the tiny kitchen, where food was kept after it had been unloaded from the trunk of their Oldsmobile sedan. How many trips up and down those cool cellar steps she took in a day must have been something, but the results were meals so remarkable that it makes my mouth water just thinking about them, some sixty years later. The cheese, summer baloney, cake and pies were left on the table, covered by a piece of cheese cloth to keep the flies away, and we were constantly snacking, from the time we got up in the morning until we went to bed. Fish caught in the lake below the cabin were immediately cleaned and fried, and added a touch of spontaneity to the meals.

This never-ending task of meal preparation, always conscientiously carried out with an attention to the proper combination of foods called for by Pennsylvania Dutch custom, was never taken for granted by any of us. We were well aware of the labor and love that went into its preparation, and were generous in our thanks to God and to Mammy for its provision.

When my mother died suddenly, my thirteen-year-old sister Lina was suddenly thrown into the role of cook for our small family (my father, three boys and herself). Every afternoon after coming home from school, she would call our grandmother and ask, "What shall I make for supper, and how do I make it?" She obviously listened well, writing down recipes and instructions dictated from memory by Mammy, because my sister became an excellent cook.

Sadly, Mammy died just a few months before Dorene and I were married, and Dorene never got to meet her; however she did send her a recipe for raisin pie, minus the amounts and the instructions, which she tried to make, unsuccessfully, several times. Fortunately, she was able to get some of the recipes my sister and my Aunt Omegene had written down over the years. Even today, the smell of one of Dorene's molasses cakes baking, made from an old recipe of Mammy's, transports me back to her kitchen in the house where she and Pappy ran a country store.

"Eats", as prepared food is called in Pennsylvania Dutch households, were the center of life for farm families such as ours. We ate all our meals at a rectangular table in the middle of the big farm kitchen. The stove was set at an angle in a special alcove on the east side of the room. Next to the alcove was a pantry, made under the steps that led to a storeroom above the kitchen. On the wall next to the steps was a piece of furniture found in all country kitchens. It was a combination pie saver, storage for flour, sugar and spices, with a large work area that slid out and on which dough was rolled and shaped into appropriate forms. Under this workspace was a storage area for pots and pans, as well as a drawer or two that included a lined breadbox. Occasionally when I wander into antique stores I will come across one of these kitchen cupboards, and it always takes me back to our kitchen and the pale green cupboard that sat in our kitchen for decades. On the north wall of the kitchen, between the two windows that overlooked the yard and garden and gave us a view of the barn and the other outbuildings, sat our refrigerator. In the early days, it was not electric; just a cabinet with heavy doors, on top of which sat a box that held ice. The cold air from the ice sank into the cavity underneath, where perishable foods were kept. When I was about four, this icebox gave way to a "proper refrigerator", with double doors and a circular cooling unit on top, where the icebox had been on the old fridge. That new, electric refrigerator served us until they day we sold the farm and auctioned off the contents.

The west side of the kitchen had a door leading to the front porch, one of the two outside entries to the kitchen, and a door leading to the rest of the house. Next to this door was a sink area, with a cupboard above and drawers below the work area and sink. A short-handled pump supplied cold water from the cistern; hot water came from the water tank in the kitchen stove, or from a tea-kettle that was always warming on it.

On the south wall of the kitchen was a door to the back porch and a window overlooking the back porch and backyard. Between the door and window had been a cupboard, but at some point a gas range, using bottled gas, was installed, primarily for summer cooking.

But the center of the kitchen was dominated by the coal stove and the kitchen table and chairs, and here we ate every meal, played cards on weekend evenings, and did homework on school nights when the table had been cleared and the dinner plates washed and put away. That kitchen table was the center of our lives, as it was for all farm families. We always sat down as a family, said grace, and ate together. Conversation at meals ranged from planning the day's activities at breakfast and reviewing them at supper, to discussions about events at school or in the community. It was at this table that the conversations leading to lessons in life and about life were initiated. Here, values were emphasized, often embroidered on by stories and yarns that made them seem less like mental medicine and more like memorable desserts.

And the big, coal stove became the focal point in the winter. When we came home from school, after trudging a half-mile through snow up to our knees, or came in from an hour or two of sleigh riding or building forts in snow banks piled high by the county snowplows, we immediately headed for the stove. We opened the oven door and, after taking off our boots and shoes, rested our feet on it, our toes just outside the oven, while we tried to balance the pain of retreating numbness with the pleasure of oven warmth caressing us. Mom always had a pot of soup warming on the back of the stove in winter, and it was where my father and the farm-hands headed after a morning of cold, outdoor work. I'm glad to see that modern homes have restored kitchens to a size where families can eat together, informally and enjoyably.

My last birthday party was planned around "eats". We had a dish from each of the countries we have lived in—*bobotie* from South Africa, *empanadas* from Chile, yoghurt and mangoes from Bangladesh. When I was explaining this to my brother over the phone a week before the event, he listened carefully and then asked, "Where's the Pennsylvania Dutch food?"

I was dumbstruck; how could I have forgotten this? It's pretty hard to come up with the ingredients for a good Pennsylvania Dutch dish at the last minute in Portland, Oregon, so we made do with sauerkraut and pork sausages ... and an empty dish with the label "Stuffed Pig's Stomach" and a note that read, "Sorry, all gone already". I prepared a program for the event, with everything listed in English and Pennsylvania Dutch. My brother and his wife helped me put together the Dutch translations, as did several menus from old Groundhog Day feasts that were tucked away in a file of family history.

There is a story here: many, many years ago my grandfather, Elmer Asry Fehnel, and twelve of his friends decided that the legend of the Groundhog needed to be captured in some way. They founded *Grundsow Lodge Nummer Ains on da Lechaw*—Groundhog Lodge Number One on the Lehigh. Lodge members met once a year, on Groundhog Day, and celebrated the day with a dinner, songs and an after dinner speaker. Everything was conducted in Pennsylvania Dutch, and if someone slipped and spoke English, they had to put a dollar in the kitty. The idea of Groundhog Lodges caught on, and now there are dozens of them scattered around Pennsylvania. While Punxsutawney Phil catches the eye of the media every year, the real celebration of this day takes place in the Lodges that my grandfather and his friends founded, and features the "eats" so central to our culture.

Above: Dick with his brother, Roger, at the beach.
Below: Dick with his father, Harold, and brother, Roger, playing catch on the farm.

Chapter 5
Free to Roam

THE FREEDOM TO ROAM BUILDS INDEPENDENCE
AND SELF-CONFIDENCE; IT ALSO ENGENDERS
EMPATHY—OR AT LEAST AN UNDERSTANDING—OF
ONE'S REALITY AND THE PEOPLE AND CRITTERS
THAT INHABIT IT.

Hardly a day goes by these days without some threat to children. At any one time in the US there are over eight hundred thousand missing children; that averages more than two thousand a day. We now have "Amber Alert", a public service announcement that breaks into broadcasts (radio and TV) when a child goes missing and there is a description of a vehicle that may be involved. Milk cartons carry the pictures of missing children. Practically every week brings the sad news of some child murdered somewhere in this country. Worldwide, the safety of children seems no better. Some governments are even involved in the trafficking of children for work, sex and military service.

What a contrast to the times when I grew up on a farm in the Lehigh Valley of eastern Pennsylvania. As a pre-schooler, I was free to roam our large yard and beyond. Granted, I was never far from the watchful eye of my big sister or my mother, but essentially I was left alone to play and explore as much as I wanted. When I began school, I walked a half-mile each way to school, usually accompanied by at least one other child my age, or a year or two older. When I got home from school, I had a few chores, but then I was free to roam again, and as I grew older the space to roam grew larger and included three wooded areas (one with a stream meandering through it), three slate quarries, acres of fields and pastures, a big barn and several other large buildings with lots of machinery, animals and tools—all essentially out of sight from my mother or anyone else who may have been told to keep an eye on me.

And then as I grew a little older, and before chores became more time consuming, summer days were spent with the two or three other boys my age from neighboring farms. Our freedom to roam was limited only by time, not by distance, nor by parental decrees, or physical boundaries. We generally had to be home for meals, or in time to do chores.

So, today, when I drive past school-bus stops, with parents hovering to collect their children and shepherd them home to secure areas protected by alarms, nannies and who knows what else, I am saddened. We have forfeited the freedom of our children to roam, to explore, to discover and to find self-confidence. When I was a child, the only invasions we heard about were military maneuvers, not the so-called "home invasions" that we hear about on the nightly local news. The only drugs we heard about were the miracle drugs produced by serious scientists in long white coats, not the scourge of drugs we hear about today, produced and peddled by shifty-eyed thugs. The only dogs in our schools were the pets that followed us, not the drug-sniffing ones that are becoming a familiar sight at many schools. Metal detectors probably hadn't been invented yet, so they certainly weren't standing guard at schoolhouse doors as they do today in many urban schools. If I left the house with a gun, it was to hunt for groundhogs, not schoolmates.

What has happened? When I went to school, America was still rural; the TV town of Mayberry actually existed in almost every county in the country, and most boys reflected the values we recognized in Opie Taylor, the boy from Mayberry in The Andy Griffith Show of the 1960s. Now, America is urban, Mayberry no longer exists, and today's Opie Taylors are lengthening their rap sheets. And with the loss of rural and small town America came the loss of the freedom of children to roam. Today, the only roaming they do is with their cell phones.

With my collie, Duke, I roamed over the farmlands and the woods, searching for discoveries that would enrich my days and give me something to dream about at night. Roaming led me to the deposit of clay, tucked under a shallow bank in the stream in the woods by the pasture. Roaming over the slate piles left by one of the quarries on our farm led me to the 10-foot slab of slate where my brother had scratched a note of a sexual conquest. Roaming led me to the discovery of an old muzzle loading rifle wrapped in burlap in a loft of one of the outbuildings on the farm, a treasure forgotten by whoever put it there.

When I was slightly older, and roamed with my companions Joe, Bobby and Donald, we explored an ice cave outside Chapman Quarry, a nearby village of Welch families who worked the slate quarries for which the village was named. When my father took the four of us to the Pennsylvania State Farm Show in January 1950, when I was twelve, the four of us were free to roam the huge multi-building complex all day, climbing on the new farm equipment, racing up and down the stairs of the arena in the biggest building any of us had ever been in, and roaming at will among the thousands of farmers and vendors who came to what was then the biggest annual event for the farm industry in the state. We had this freedom because there were no threats to our safety at that time.

Such freedom granted us by our fathers was not special or unique. It was how they and their fathers were raised as well. In our America, the adventures of Huck Finn could be lived by boys our age. My distant relative, Daniel Boone, would not have gained the skills that made him famous if he were bound by the security blankets parents feel obliged to throw over their children today.

I'm not just talking about the physical sense of roaming free; our freedom to roam mentally—to imagine, to dream—also seems to be in sharp contrast to the circumstances of today. Today's children really are "programmed" in the worst sense of the word. Their free time—the time I had to imagine, to make up games, circumstances, situations— is filled with activities that someone else has imagined for them. We listened to radio and imagined the Lone Ranger and Tonto racing through sagebrush, chasing the bad guys. Today's kids watch TV; they don't need to imagine anything. Even the canned laughter cues them. Idle time is spent with a "gameboy" or a video game—following the imagined action someone else has scripted for them. Even when they aren't playing video games, they are plugged into some form of sound system, listening to someone else's imagined version of reality or spending hours on the internet in a virtual reality that seems less and less like the real world with each passing day.

We have a fifteen-year-old nephew who occasionally comes to visit for several days at a time. We introduced a new rule on a recent visit; no "gameboy", no TV, no walkman, no Ipod. Initially he just sat for long periods of time staring at the blank TV screen. He literally did not know what to do to entertain himself. He had no "imaginative pulse". We began to cure that by going to the library, and by getting him to help me clean out the garage and paint the floor. But it really is scary to witness the dulling effects of a dozen years of not having to initiate creative, playful thinking.

The other thing about the programmed lives today's children and young adults lead is that the programming seems to be isolating. It directs our attention inward or towards some object (the monitor) and isolates us from the interaction with others that can take creativity and imagination to new levels. Eroding the freedom to roam, physically and mentally, is driving us apart as individuals, as neighbors and as a nation. We are no longer a melting pot, a nation of people rubbing shoulders. We are increasingly a nation of self-centered individuals, surfing channels and the internet in isolated "safety" rather than engaging with each other. It takes a national tragedy to shake us from this stupor, and unfortunately, that effect is only temporary. And as we become increasingly comfortable in our isolation, we wonder why our nation seems to be losing touch with reality.

While the rest of the world seems united in trying to confront global warming, our current government pretends it doesn't exist. While the rest of the world struggles to find ways to accommodate diversity, we insist that the American way is the only way. When an American city drowns in the aftermath of one of the worst hurricanes, many of its citizens begging for assistance on national TV, our leaders go on vacation or fund raise for the next political campaign, assuming someone else will come to the rescue.

The freedom to roam builds independence and self-confidence; it also engenders empathy—or at least an understanding—of one's reality and the people and critters that inhabit it. This is a gradual process, and can and should be taught. Every spring Mrs Bossard would take all the students of Gravers School on a half-day outing in a valley near the school that passed through farmlands and woods, with several streams. She would give an assignment to each grade to study different plants and insect life, and to be able to describe the environment in which these were found. To the older students she would have them observe the relationship between the farms and the woods, and whether the farmers were trying to keep a balance between the two. Since we were all farm kids, we thought we knew all the answers, but soon learned how important it was to see the details, and then to try to "connect the dots" between the details and the larger picture. Slowly our understanding of ecology grew. By the time I was in 8th grade I was able to write a detailed paper, complete with photographs, of the problems of erosion and pollution of a stream that supplied the drinking water to the town of Bath. I earned a Boy Scout merit badge for the paper, and it was printed in the local newspaper.

Undoubtedly, one could find wonderful examples of similar things being done by some students today. The movie *Paper Clips* is an excellent example of such an endeavor. But, when one tries to get a sense of a national attitude, or national practices, one gets the feeling that what our children are being encouraged to do, largely by their peers and by the activities they see on MTV and the other sources of their cues to "in" behavior, are not the kinds of mental and physical roaming that will engender an empathy or an understanding of their environment. Nor, for that matter, does much of prime-time TV. If anything, most of the so-called reality TV shows demonstrate how dysfunctional our families have become and how self-centered our Gen-Xers are. The shopping hysteria over the release of new technology toys, such as the XBox360 or the Ipod with video capability only reinforce this stereotypical behavior.

What are the values today's media reinforce? What are the lessons being espoused? Do they affirm the same values and the same lessons that were manifested in "the Greatest Generation" or those of us born a little too late to be a part of that generation of selfless men and women who literally helped save the world from totalitarianism? I don't think so, and I struggle to understand how we let these things slip away from our national consciousness and our national agenda. Sure, our politicians call for a return to "family values", but they have been redefined in ways that stand in stark contrast to the family values practiced in many farm families and, for that matter, many first and second generation immigrant families that lived in America's cities around the time of World War II. One only has to read biographies such as *Flags of Our Fathers* or *A Long Way from Home: Growing Up in the American Heartland in the Forties and Fifties* to know that things have changed in terms of how we as children were expected to behave—what the values were that our parents believed in and expected us to believe in. These changes have resulted in our children's loss of the freedom to roam, a loss understandably, at least in the short run, of the fears of parents about roaming, whether it is in the neighborhood or in cyberspace.

Chapter 6
The Family Implodes

ONE LESSON I LEARNED WAS A LESSON NOT JUST
ABOUT SURVIVAL, BUT ABOUT WINNING
IN THE FACE OF OVERWHELMING ODDS.

Graduation from Allentown High School, 1956.
(From left to right) Robert (brother), father, Dick.

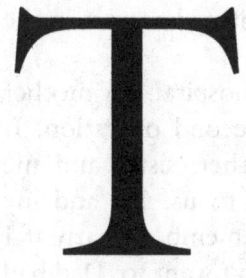The last conversation I remember having with my mother was in our outhouse. I was just nine years old, capable of "going" by myself, but she asked me to accompany her. It was a late autumn day, and the sunlight shone through the only window on the left side of the outhouse. The honeysuckle arbor still covered some of the window, casting shadows on her face. She pulled me close to her as she sat, and told me that she was going to go to the hospital in a few days and wanted me to promise that I would listen to my sister.

"When will you come home?" I asked.

She paused. "When the doctor says it's OK." Her reply was somewhat tentative; she must have had a premonition that coming home may not have been likely.

"Why must you go to the hospital?" I didn't remember her being sick at all, so it seemed strange that she was going.

"Dr Brong says I need an operation to fix something that sometimes goes wrong with women."

"Oh." I didn't have the slightest idea what she was talking about. What can go wrong with a 37-year-old farm woman who was the picture of health, teaching us to sing good ol' Southern songs as we helped her to can peaches, make sauerkraut and churn butter, among other chores that we happily helped her with. She was a Southerner by birth and still kept close ties with her Southern relatives, as attested by our annual pilgrimage to the Marshall Family Reunion in Maryland. She had adapted well to the cuisine and temperament of the happy Pennsylvania Dutch, as our branch of the Pennsylvania Dutch was known, in contrast to the somber, plain Dutch as the Amish were known. So, making sauerkraut, chow-chow and other Dutch dishes had become second nature to her, and we kids could help with many of these chores, during which she taught us the songs of the South, the songs of her youth.

"Run along, now, and remember your promise." She gave me an extra tight hug, and seemed to cling to me as I must have clung to her a thousand times.

I'm sure we must have spoken again before she left for Allentown General Hospital, but I only remember that brief conversation in the outhouse as our last. I vaguely remember visiting her once in the hospital, but don't remember any conversation.

A few days later my father got a call from the hospital. My mother had taken a turn for the worse, following a second operation. It looked pretty grim. He called my older brother, sister and me together in the kitchen and relayed the news to us. He and my brother quickly left for the hospital. I don't remember clearly if I was given the choice of going, but I knew I didn't want to. Dad had made it clear that it might be the last time we'd see our mother alive. Maybe I thought that if I didn't go, she couldn't die. But she did.

The next time I saw her was at the viewing in Schlisler's Funeral Home in Northampton. Almost sixty years later I can still smell the heavy scent of flowers as we walked in the viewing room. My father, brother, sister and I walked to the coffin together. I wound up standing next to her face. At nine years of age, I was the right height to look directly at her face, in profile, as she lay in the coffin. She looked so peaceful, just like she was sleeping. A slight smile on her face. My mother looked a bit like Faye Dunaway, the actress. A high forehead, high cheekbones, sandy blondish hair, thin, fine bones and soft, loving eyes.

I can remember thinking how weird this all was. Then we had to sit in the front row while all the extended family and friends came in, walked to the coffin, paused a bit, then came by and whispered condolences to us. Uncle Walter, the Carpenters Union steward, in his typical rough way, pulled my hair and shook a finger at me, whispering in his gruff voice that I would have to be good now and listen to my sister. Jesus, did he know about the talk in the outhouse? My sister, Lina, was thirteen. She sat next to me at the viewing. Her brown eyes seemed puffy from crying. Her curly brown hair, which usually bounced, seemed restrained, awed by the setting. My father kept wiping his eyes with a handkerchief. During the last few days I had seen him cry for the first time in my life. It was a shock. The whole thing was a shock and I wanted it to be over, to get back to the way things were. I wanted Mom to wake up.

The next day was the funeral at Zion Stone Church in Kreidersville. It was the day before Thanksgiving. Talk about bad timing. It was a cold, windy day, though the sun was shining brightly. After the service in the church—this church where I had spent almost every

Sunday of my young life, as my name on the perfect attendance roster proved—we followed the coffin out of the church, then walked through the cemetery to the section where the Fehnels and Reinhards and distant relatives were buried. I didn't know it then, but it was to be the first of several winter days over the next decade or more that I was to spend in that damn cemetery. Why do the Fehnels always die in the winter I asked myself more than once? The church and the cemetery sit high on a hill in the farmlands of Northampton County, only about twenty miles from the Appalachian Mountains, and on winter days, cold wind comes down from the mountains, sending a chill through the cemetery that gloves, scarves and topcoats can't compete with. It is the coldness of Death amplified.

We buried my mother that cold November day, and life was never the same after that for any of us.

Two months later my father was in Allentown General Hospital, looking up at Dr Trexler, the same surgeon who had operated on our mother.

"Don't worry, Harold; it'll be OK," he assured Dad.

I would have said, "Like hell you'll operate on me!"

But Dad didn't have a choice. He had a badly ruptured stomach ulcer and had lost lots of blood. This was not the time for being picky about who operated on him.

He came home from the hospital several weeks later, with a full-time nurse in tow. Her name was Velma Irene Doncsecz—Irene, as she became known to us—and she was to stay with him until she died of cancer eleven years later. Although they didn't marry until just before she died, she soon ruled the household as though she had the rights and authority of the stepmother. Within a month or two of her being there it became clear that she was the controlling influence on my father. As the months and years went by she isolated our little family from the rest of the extended family. And within our little family she drove each of us away as soon as we had the means to support ourselves. My older brother, seventeen and a senior in high school when our mother died, left to live with our parental grandparents shortly after Irene was on the scene, and even before he graduated from high school. In the brief time that he spent in the house with Irene and our father, his life was made intolerably miserable, even though he had managed to run the farm while Dad was hospitalized and during the early days of his home-recuperation. After he left, rescued by our grandparents, years went by before he and my father talked to each other, and they never reached a point where my brother forgave our father for choosing Irene over our family, and permitting her to mistreat his children.

Her mistreatment took many forms. She stole clothing or anything that had value to us. On occasions she refused to allow us to eat with the rest of the family. She taught our little brother, only three when she came into our lives, to say "I hate you" to my brother, sister and myself, and to spy on us and tell her where we might have hidden anything she might want to take from us. She lied about our activities; she hid or destroyed mail addressed to us. When my sister cooked for us, Irene sometimes threw out what Lina had just made—not because it was bad, but just to be mean. Through all this, our father never took issue with any of her actions. So, our love for him turned to confusion and then to hatred.

My sister left home as soon as she graduated from business college, had a job and could afford an apartment, which she shared with a friend. It was years before she and our father spoke, but after Irene died and our father married for the third time, they were able to establish a comfortable, though somewhat distant, relationship. It was years before she overcame her guilt at having abandoned my younger brother and me to this wretched household.

I reached the end of my rope early in my senior year in high school, and moved in with my brother and his family until I left for college. Like my older brother, I never really reconciled with my father, though we found a little space for brief visits. We all resented the fact that he had abandoned us to her malicious control, and never stood up for our rights.

As I look back on this situation from the perspective of more than fifty years, several mysteries remain. Not only were we, the children, unable to understand why our father behaved the way he did, it is just as odd that we, now adults with families of our own, have never talked about those horrible years. Nor was the situation ever discussed with us by my paternal grandparents, who clearly knew what was going on down on the farm. Linda Hunt, in her reconstruction of the amazing story of Helga Estby, discusses why families keep secrets such as ours. Often it is out of shame, and each of us children had a different sense of shame than the others, but the effect was the same. We waited for the right moment to leave home and then we sealed the shame in memories that lay buried until I started writing about it as part of the larger story of my life.

I have cited the lessons learned at Gravers School, and some of the lessons learned growing up on the farm. But perhaps the most important lesson learned was through my relationship with Irene. It would be an understatement to say that I hated her. She is the only person I have ever consciously thought about murdering. And when I realized I couldn't do that, I thought about ending my own life. And when I couldn't do that, I learned to cope—to escape through reading, through Luther League activities, through work, through any means that kept me sane over the eight years I endured her reign over our household.

One lesson I learned was a lesson not just about survival, but about winning in the face of overwhelming odds.

Irene kept cutting off our "life lines"—support that might be forthcoming from extended family and close family friends. Not only that, she tried to make life as miserable as she could by demeaning our efforts, and by depriving us of all means of comfort. I made it through junior high school and part of high school with two shirts and two pairs of trousers. Not that we were poor; she just kept stealing any clothes that we were given or that our father bought. She had done this to my brother and sister as well. She was a kleptomaniac. She continued to work on and off as a private nurse, carefully choosing her clients. She only worked for people she could steal from without fear of being caught. She stole from them regularly and stored her stash in a room she kept locked.

The tragedy was that our father turned a blind eye to this, and to the deeper rifts that she created in the family. This was why we developed a hatred for him. We could never understand why he made this choice. But he had and we had to endure it as long as we could. My "sentence" was longer than those of my older brother and sister, but I had learned how to cope and carve out some breathing space. A turning point in that process occurred when I was about thirteen or fourteen. One morning Irene and I had a shouting match in the kitchen on the farm. It had something to do with my chore of cleaning the ashes from the wood and coal stove in the kitchen, and bringing in a new bucket of coal. I don't remember why or how the argument started, but at some point Irene either hit me or shoved me.

My response was quick: a right cross, flush on her chin. Angelo Dundee would have been proud of the speed and accuracy of the punch. It knocked her onto her butt on the kitchen floor. From then on she kept her distance. She reported the incident to my dad, who caught up with me later that day, after I had come home from school and was working in our machine shop. Sharp words were exchanged at close range, and he moved towards me menacingly. That practiced right cross again came into action. I didn't knock him down, but when his head snapped back his glasses fell to the shop floor. In the time it took to collect them and put them on he must have decided that a fight was not in our best interests, so he made a threatening warning about ever hitting him or Irene again. I replied that if one of them ever laid a hand on me again, there would be more than one punch—that frankly I would beat the shit out of either of them. He knew I meant it, and knew I probably could do it. Years of lifting bales of hay and sacks of potatoes had given me strength well beyond my years, and taking up boxing in PE at junior high school had given me the confidence I needed to know how to use this strength.

Why our father never came to the defense of his children; why he allowed Irene to do the evil things she did were questions we have never been able to answer. Was it sexual control? Was it financial control? Was it the powerlessness that sometimes accompanies love? Once, early in the relationship, when Irene left in a huff for several days, my sister, brother and I confronted Dad about the destruction she was causing in the family. We said it was a problem that he alone could solve. He acknowledged that; then did nothing and she returned with more authority than ever.

His unwillingness to solve the problem with Irene remains a source of irony and mystery to us to this day because our father was an inventive problem-solver. He used to say that laziness, not necessity, was the mother of invention and during the winter months on the farm he would invent pieces of farm equipment that were labor savers. He invented a double row potato-digging machine. Four people sat on the back of this machine and sorted good potatoes from bad and from rocks, weeds and other field debris. Then the potatoes went up a conveyor belt onto a truck and when the truck was full, another truck took its place while the first one emptied its load in the huge cellar where the crop was stored. This machine essentially made the dozens of people hired to pick potatoes redundant. He also invented a machine that hooked on the side of a truck and picked up bales of hay or straw and lifted them up to the back of the truck where they could be stacked. Two people could clear a field of baled hay or straw in a fraction of the time it would have taken three or four people.

These were just two of the many problems he solved by using his brain and hands. But he wouldn't solve the biggest problem of all facing our family. He wouldn't even try, despite the obvious damage being done. One by one family traditions fell by the way side. Christmas dinners at my grandparents' home stopped. Summer vacations spent helping the customers in their country store stopped. Wonderful summer weekends at the family cabin at Lake Minisink in the Poconos, which I can still recall with great detail, and great fondness, stopped. Going to the Grange picnics stopped. Instead, we began to spend Sundays with Irene's family.

The Doncsecz' were first-generation immigrants. They were Windish, part of the Windish migration from Prekmurje, a mountainous region in eastern Slovenia, who came to Bethlehem, Pennsylvania to work in the steel mills. The family was large, eight sons and two daughters, and was ruled over by a tyrant of a father who spoke no English. His wife had refused to come to America, so he took up with another woman who bore all of his children, then died.

As usually happens under tyranny, the children, all adults still living at home except for Irene and one or two brothers, showed their unhappiness through aggression towards each other and particularly towards outsiders, which meant my father and whichever of his children he had brought with him to visit on Sundays. So, my Sundays which had been spent happily playing with two cousins my own age in my grandparents home, which always had sounds of laughter echoing through it, were now spent in this bizarre environment, where people shouted at one another, or avoided each other, and where an uneasy quiet hung over everything and where there were no children.

We stopped going to Zion Stone Church. No more stopping at Schaffer's Bakery in the little town of Bath after church for freshly made molasses cookies and bread. Irene dragged us to her church, Christ Lutheran in Allentown. It was where the wealthy Lutheran families of Allentown went to church, and she had pretensions that we belonged there. I don't think any other farm families went there. I felt out of place, and I know my father did, too, but he allowed us to be taken there every Sunday.

Eventually, I turned this situation to my advantage. But in the meantime the combination of Irene's influence and my father's problem-solving proclivities led to a situation I had never imagined. We sold the family farm. The hundred years that Fehnels had farmed these beautiful, productive fields came to an end. The dairy herd of purebred Guernseys we had carefully built over a decade was sold to the highest bidder. The tractors I had learned to drive with the precision that all farm boys attain sat silenced. The barn where I had literally spent most of my life up to the age of sixteen, where so many of life's mysteries were revealed and life's joys were embraced, and from whose huge timbers I had swung on ropes, as a pirate, a cowboy, Tarzan, a soldier escaping Nazis SS troops—this barn now closed its doors to me and I never again entered its world. Duke, the collie with whom I had roamed fields, woods and streams—my hunting companion, my confessor, my counselor when days fighting Irene really got to me—was left on the farm and I never saw him again.

My father had figured out that moving up the potato production chain, from growing them to selling them, processed as raw French fries to restaurants, school and hospital cafeterias, was better business. So, we sold the farm and in the middle of my sophomore year I was reluctantly transformed from a farm boy to a city kid. Talk about a fish out of water! We moved to Allentown, first to a row house a block away from Christ Lutheran Church, then to a fancier house in a better part of town.

And it was in this setting that I was able to begin turning things to my advantage. Forced to go to Christ Lutheran, I got involved in Luther League, the Lutheran Church's activity group for teenagers. It became my support group, and its adult leaders, Wilbur and Betty Rader, became my source of guidance. They knew of my home situation, and through their encouragement and support I weathered the situation until I made my break for freedom. It was Wilbur who met me two blocks from my house, with my one suitcase of belongings and drove me to my brother's house when I ran away from home in my senior year of high school. It was Wilbur who counseled me on applying for scholarships, and when I was awarded three, he helped me think through the options. I accepted an NROTC scholarship that allowed me to choose from among fifty-two universities, and he guided me towards selecting the University of Washington, not because of its strong engineering program (I thought I wanted to be an engineer), but because it was as far away from Allentown as I could get, and would give me an opportunity to start my life unburdened by the past. A clean slate; a new beginning; new lessons to learn. Although I kept open the communication with my father, unlike my brother who wouldn't speak to him for years, my father was never again a factor in the decisions I made throughout the rest of my life.

July 1959.
Dorene and Dick, newly engaged.

Chapter 7
A New Beginning

YOU LEARNED THAT TEAMWORK REALLY IS AT THE HEART OF SUCCESSFUL EFFORTS, AND THAT IF YOU HOLD BACK FROM A TOTAL COMMITMENT TO A TEAM EFFORT YOU'LL PROBABLY PAY A HEAVY PRICE FOR IT SOONER OR LATER.

The wheels of the propeller-driven United airliner touched down for the sixth time that day. I was weary and glad to be at the end of my travels. At the start of the day, when I boarded the plane in Allentown, Pennsylvania, I had never flown before. Now, there I was, dragging myself and a carry-on off the plane in Seattle, Washington, after stops in Pittsburgh, St Louis, Denver and Portland. I was about to enter the University of Washington as a freshman, three thousand miles from Allentown, Pennsylvania.

During the stopover in Portland, I had left the plane to meet briefly with my great-aunt Olive and great-uncle "Golden" Davis, who lived in Tigard, a suburb of Portland. I had met them ten years earlier, when they drove east to visit relatives in Virginia, Maryland and Pennsylvania. In a way, they were partly responsible for my deciding to attend the University of Washington, in Seattle. As children, every year at Christmas each of us received a book from Aunt Olive and Uncle Golden. They were always illustrated books that transported us to magical places. Every year we looked forward to those Christmas presents move than anything else, not just because they were frequently the most expensive present we received, but because of the hours of enjoyment we got from them, and the luxury of being able to travel in our imagination to far off places.

One of my favorite books was one in which Donald Duck visited Latin America. It made quite an impression on me; years later, when I crossed the Panama Canal and traveled down the West Coast of South America to Chile, I remembered Donald's adventures in these strange lands, and silently thanked Aunt Olive and Uncle Golden again for their gift. So, when the time came to pick a college, not only was I pushed by the tragic unhappiness that had befallen our family, I was pulled by the magic of far away places, and didn't hesitate to leave the Lehigh Valley.

Seattle was to be my new home. I took a taxi, another first in my life that day, from SeaTac Airport to the address on the card I clutched tightly in my hand. I was panicky about losing the card, because it was my only connection to anything in Seattle. When the taxi dropped me off at Rofcre House, on 18th Avenue in the U District, I really didn't know what to expect. The University of Washington (UW) didn't have any dormitories for men yet (they were to open a year later). I couldn't afford to join a fraternity, so I had selected one of the Independent Men's Residences from the housing information sent to me. These residences were organized in a co-operative, but each was a separate facility and the six houses were scattered around Greek Row, north of the campus.

The house looked like it hadn't been painted in a number of years, and the front yard looked neglected. So, I was somewhat apprehensive as I mounted the steps and rang the bell. After what seemed like an eternity, during which my anxiety level went up several notches, the door opened and I was greeted warmly by the house president, Jamison Akina, a Hawaiian (and another first for me that day). Jamison apologized for my having to wait, and explained that he and some of the other house members were downstairs in the dining-room cleaning it up after a summer of neglect.

I didn't know it at the time, but the men who came to live in Rofcre House were to become a band of brothers that stayed together even when we moved as a "house" and took over one floor of the new dormitory a year later. It was the most heterogeneous group I could have imagined. Not only were their several Hawaiians, and African Americans, there were men of Swedish, Finnish, Danish, Russian and Asian extraction. But I was the only Pennsylvania Dutchman—for the first time in my life, I was a member of an ethnic minority.

There were about forty men, and we actually had two houses, side-by-side, that constituted Rofcre House. (The odd name of the house, I learned, was an acronym made up from the name of the founder of a universal co-operative movement, Robert Owen, and a place name in England associated with the great man's life.) At least a half dozen of the men were veterans, attending the university on the GI Bill. Several others had NROTC scholarships, as I did. One thing we all had in common was the fact that we all came from poorer, working-class families. None were graduates of Seattle high schools, which in a sense made us all outsiders from the cliquey provincialism of the UW.

As the weeks and months went by, this outsider identity bound us closer together. Of course, beer helped. I was soon learning how to make home brew as I helped Forrest Tucker, the ex-Marine who lived in the house, brew a case at a time. The nightly card games in the living-room also had a bonding effect, as well as providing me with a few extra dollars a month, since I quickly mastered the game of Hearts, and there was always a Hearts game going on for a penny a point.

We had a basketball court behind the smaller house, and this not only provided an opportunity to work off some of the stress that developed as we confronted our new reality, it was also to provide the key to my future wife. More about that later.

Perhaps the most stressful aspect of the new circumstances we faced was the fact that we were now in a new league academically. Many of us had graduated near the top of our high school graduation classes (I was tenth out of a graduating class of 811), and some, like me, hardly broke a sweat in getting those top grades. I had also had a job in high school, was involved in athletics, and had a leadership role in the Luther League. But suddenly we were in classes where everybody was at least as smart as we were, and quite a few were a lot smarter. Having never had to study very hard in high school, I had appalling study skills, and slowly but surely I began to slip behind. Unfortunately, my response was to seek escape. That had worked for me in my abysmal home life. It seemed to work for a while, but it turned out to be an illusion.

By the end of winter quarter, I was in deep academic trouble. So I did the next logical thing: I changed majors from Engineering to Far Eastern Affairs. Adding to my academic woes was another reality; the girl whom I had developed a deep affection for in high school—whose parents came close to being surrogate parents to me—seemed to be growing more remote in the letters we exchanged. Pat and I had been practically inseparable during our senior year. Her parents knew of my home situation, and were glad when I moved out to live with my brother. They admired my independence and my maturity, and gave me lots of encouragement when I left the Lehigh Valley to attend the University of Washington. So, as the letters from Pat lost their passion, I decided to make use of spring break and head home to Allentown, hitch-hiking my way on military aircraft. By wearing my midshipman's uniform and carrying documents proving that I was a student at the University of Washington, I was able to get a seat on military planes if there was space. As soon as finals were over in March 1957, several of us drove from Seattle to the Bay area of California, where they dropped me at Travis Air Force base. Within a few hours I was on my way, free, to the East Coast.

When I got home I found that the coolness from Pat in her letters was worse in person. It was over. She had decided that she didn't want to spend the next four years playing a waiting game and missing out on much of the social life of her own college experience. So, I was forced to face another lesson in life: absence does not necessarily make the heart grow fonder. It had been my decision to go so far away, and now I had to pay the price for it.

I almost paid the ultimate price for that trip home. Ten days later, when it was time to return to Seattle, I was unable to find a military flight West. So I called a relative in Baltimore who sold aviation fuel to several of the large military bases on the East Coast. Within a day he had a flight for me to Arizona. He took me to the flight hanger at an Air Force base outside of Baltimore, where I learned there were actually two aircraft going to the Air Force's graveyard for surplus aircraft. This was to be the last flight for these two birds—B-17s, as I recall. One of the planes had four or five GIs hitching a ride in the back; the other had no passengers, just the crew chief. Since I had had little sleep during my hectic vacation days, I opted for the empty plane. Little did I realize that I had just made a fateful choice.

The planes took off and we flew in a loose convoy. Since I was essentially alone in the back, I was given a pair of earphones and a microphone, so the crew could communicate with me. Our first refueling stop was Memphis Naval Air Station, which shared an airfield with the commercial airport serving Memphis. Somewhere over Virginia or Tennessee we ran into very heavy weather. The plane was tossed about in a thunderstorm like a toy. At some point we lost radio contact with the other plane, but we continued on our way. When we finally reached Memphis, the terrible storm was behind us, but we faced a new problem; our landing gear wouldn't descend! The storm had obviously shaken the plane so hard that the landing gear system had been disrupted. As we circled the airport, the crew chief and I tried to crank down the gear manually, but that didn't work either. So, the ground crew at Memphis prepared a runway for a crash-landing on a foam pad.

In the back of the plane, the crew chief laid a fire axe between us and said, "As soon as we stop, you take out that window (the Plexiglas covering over what had been a side turret for a machine gun) and get ready to hit the deck. This baby is likely to catch on fire."

"Damn," I said to myself. "I should have taken the other plane."

We came in for the landing, and I could see the fire trucks racing down the runway behind us. Ever so gently the pilot put the plane on the foam pad and kept it there as we screeched to a halt. I was out of my harness, axe in hand when the copilot shouted over the intercom, "Don't break the window, we're OK, no fire, no fire!"

As I recall, we had to climb out an opening in the cockpit, and the ground crew took us over to the flight shack where we could settle our nerves. I'm sure I wasn't the only guy with the shakes on that short ride.

We were surprised that the other plane wasn't already on the ground, and the pilot asked the crew in the flight shack where it was. There was a very long pause, as the crew behind the flight ops desk looked at each other and then at us.

"It went down in the storm. As far as we know there were no survivors."

I can remember almost vomiting when I heard that. The next hour or so was a total blank to me. Finally the pilot came up to me; he had my duffle bag, along with the duffle bags of the others.

"We're going to spend a couple of days here while they fix the landing gear problem. You're welcome to join us."

I looked across at the commercial planes standing at the terminal, and then at our heap, now being towed to a maintenance hangar.

"Sir, if you don't mind, I'll take a commercial flight from here. I have to get back to classes." While the last statement was true, it wasn't the main reason I couldn't see myself climbing back into that plane. He gave me an understanding smile, shook my hand, and I swung the duffle bag over my shoulder and headed for the exit and a taxi to safety. Another lesson: things that are free can turn out to be a really bad deal.

In spring quarter at the UW, after six or seven months of rain, all hell broke loose. The Greeks seemed to have endless parties, and since we were in the middle of Greek Row, with one sorority across the street and another across the alley behind our house, and a fraternity next to our main house, we also got the fever. Years later, when I was a faculty member at the University of Oregon, the movie *Animal House* was made on our campus. When I saw the movie I realized that Rofcre House in the Spring Term of 1957 could have been the prototype for that insanely funny movie.

The social highlight for Rofcre House was the annual Spring Costume Ball. To call it a Ball is to insult the thousands of dances held at universities and other social institutions around the world each year, attended by well-behaved young men and women. The Rofcre House Spring Ball was straight out of something planned and executed by Bacchus. It was nothing short of a drunken orgy. We prepared the house by removing all the furniture from the living- and dining-rooms and replacing it with mattresses. Most of the guys had dates, and most of the mattresses were used before the night was out. I was a little shy; my date and I went back to my room, where I learned another lesson in life—too much alcohol inhibits both male and female sexual performance. We both passed out on my bed, only to be rudely awakened when my room-mate and his date came stumbling in.

The guys that didn't have dates invented their own fun and games, and the highlight was when Phil Mahoney, the senior journalism student who had been enrolled for something like thirty consecutive quarters but couldn't graduate because he kept failing the Reserve Officer Training Course (ROTC), decided that he and his room-mate Stacey, a one-eyed guy who had had crippling polio as a child and walked with crutches, decided it was time to take a ride around the neighborhood.

They were both drunk, but that didn't stop Stacey from driving. "In that case," Phil slurred, "I'll ride shotgun." They were accompanied to their car by a small crowd of revellers who couldn't believe it when Phil produced a sword from the trunk of the car (he had "borrowed" it earlier in the day from one of the cadets in the house who used it as commander of his ROTC Drill Team), and with great drama threw off his toga and stood naked on the running board on the passenger's side and yelled at Stacey to get the show rolling. As the car weaved down 18th Street, Phil swung his sword wildly, lopping off the antennas of as many cars he could get a good swing at. Unfortunately for Phil, the very last car on the block was a police car, and the officers inside didn't take too kindly to having their antenna shorn off. Needless to say, Phil was a guest of the City of Seattle, Wallingford District Police Station, for the rest of the night and most of the next day. Somehow, Stacey avoided being hauled in. When Phil came home the next day he was greeted as a returning war hero.

The US Navy owned my college summers. It was part of the scholarship deal; eight weeks on a "summer cruise" every summer, getting an orientation to the various branches of service within the Department of the Navy, as well as meeting other midshipmen from the other 51 universities that participated in the Naval ROTC program.

The first summer (1957) we all converged on Newport News, Virginia, where we became part of the largest Naval Task Force organized since the end of World War II. Most of the upperclassmen were assigned to the cruisers and destroyers in the Task Force; most of us between our freshman and sophomore years were assigned to the USS Wisconsin, BB64, a battleship in the same class as the Missouri. There were over three thousand of us on this floating city, crammed into the most inconceivable and inhospitable spaces. Our destination was Valparaiso, Chile, with stops in Panama and Guantánamo Bay, Cuba.

We quickly learned about ship life, having to stand watches and perform all the functions carried out on a US man-of-war. There were countless gunnery exercises, which were actually quite exciting when the mammoth sixteen-inch cannons on the Wisconsin roared to life. My gunnery position was on an anti-aircraft gun on the port side of the ship. In the midst of our pretend battles it was a noisy spot, but provided a good view of what was going on all over the ship—when you had time to watch.

The most exciting part of the first leg of the cruise was going through the Panama Canal. The Wisconsin barely fit—we had six inches of clearance on either side of the ship as we passed through the locks. Many of us were able to get off the ship to watch as the mechanical donkeys slowly eased it through the locks. On this first passage through the Canal, there was no "liberty", that would come on the return trip. So, as soon as we were in the Pacific the Task Force headed south. Our crossing of the equator was celebrated in the traditional way, with King Neptune and all his attendants making sure we went through an appropriate hazing. All polliwogs—those who had never crossed the equator—had to crawl through a garbage-strewn canvas sleeve, while a fire hose sprayed you with seawater. When you made it through this, you had to kiss King Neptune's bellybutton. And then you were a shellback—a veteran of crossing the equator. Surprisingly, many of the ship's regular crew had never crossed the equator before, so for a day at least, we midshipmen were not the only ones on the bottom of the social hierarchy.

Crossing the Tropic of Capricorn brought welcome relief from the sweltering heat aboard ship that we had endured since leaving Virginia. It had become so bad that many of us took to dragging our bedrolls topside and sleeping on deck. But now, as we headed into the winter of the southern hemisphere, nights were spent below deck and days saw us starting to layer our limited clothing inventory in order to keep warm as the wind battered us on the open decks.

The arrival of the US Navy Task Force in the port of Valparaiso, Chile, was the biggest event ever in this city. To celebrate, local newspapers reported that prostitutes all the way from Argentina had converged on "Valpo". They were there to entertain the Navy regulars. As officers and gentlemen in training, the midshipmen were bussed to Santiago, where we were guests at numerous balls, and given the opportunity to meet with the daughters of the social elite. I met a sweet, attractive young woman who was better able to make herself understood in English than I could in Spanish. We were appropriately chaperoned, and on my second day in Santiago I was invited to her home for lunch, in a small town outside Santiago. Her father was a retired military officer who now ran a wine store, and after lunch I left with two bottles of Chile's finest, cleverly wrapped up in a leather pillow pouch that adorned a special place in my grandparents living-room for decades afterward. The wine, however, never made it off the ship. A friend and I drank the bottle of white wine somewhere between Panama and Cuba, and the bottle of red wine had an ending worth relating.

As the Task Force sailed into Newport News on our return, we all had our duffle bags packed and were ready to disembark for the last time. The bottle of red wine was carefully wrapped in the leather pouch and that was wrapped in some of my dirty clothes. We dropped anchor and waited ... and waited ... and waited. Three thousand midshipmen on the Wisconsin were getting very restless. We could see other ships in the Task Force sending their midshipmen ashore, but for some reason we were still standing by.

Finally, there was an announcement over the ship's intercom system. Someone had removed the two brass stars from the Admiral's barge, and no one was getting off the ship until they were returned! We thought that was pretty funny—a midshipman taking a very memorable trophy home from this unforgettable trip. But apparently the Admiral didn't think it was funny. More delay ... he wasn't blinking. Then another announcement—all midshipmen were to return to their quarters, with their duffle bags. What a hassle that was—it was bad enough heaving them up from five decks below once, but now having to carry them down again in the heat of the midday, and then back up again was not fun. When we were all standing by our bunks, another announcement—there would be a compartment-by-compartment search until the stars were found, starting on my deck! We were to unpack our bags and put all our belongings on our bunks. I was panic struck. The guy in the next bunk said, "you better get rid of the bottle of wine, Fehnel, or you'll spend the rest of the summer scrubbing the deck on the Whiskey," as the US Wisconsin was fondly dubbed.

I could hear the search starting in the compartment next to ours so I grabbed the leather pouch and started for the head, when the bottle of wine slipped out of the pouch and smashed on the steel deck. Immediately our little compartment was filled with the bouquet of cabernet sauvignon. For a second or two no one moved, then all hell broke loose. Suddenly dirty T-shirts were mopping up the wine, and aftershave was being sloshed all over the floor. I picked up the glass in a T-shirt and dumped it in a wastebasket in the shower room on the other side of our compartment. We braced ourselves for the search party, knowing there would be raised eyebrows and pointed questions over the wet floor and the strange mix of odors.

But the search party never came into our compartment. The stars were found in the compartment next to ours. A UW classmate had done the deed and knowing he couldn't get away with it, put the stars where they could be found, without revealing who took them.

And so, I wasn't able to drink a fine bottle of Chilean red until eight years later, when my wife, daughter and I moved to Chile for a wonderful two-year stay.

The second summer cruise was designed to give us an orientation to Naval Air and Marine Corps. Half of the midshipmen of the Class of 1960 were given orders to converge on the US Naval Air Station at Corpus Christi, Texas, for four weeks, while the other half got to play being Marines at Little Creek, Virginia, and then we would swap locations. The west coast universities were to go to Texas first, but we didn't need to be there until after the 4th of July. Two of my UW classmates and I pooled our travel money, bought a used VW beetle with a sunroof and headed towards Corpus Christi by way of Mexico City!

It was a very memorable trip, especially our morning on the beach at Mazatlan. Since we were traveling on a very tight budget, we slept on a quiet stretch of beach somewhere north of the main part of town. In the morning we were awakened by the sounds of hammers meeting nails on a building under construction just on the other side of the road from our beachfront accommodation.

The beach was spectacular; huge waves crashing onto the surf just yards away from where we were. It was also deserted, which we attributed to the early hour. Jim Bicknell and I decided to go for a swim to freshen up, but Bruce Hutchinson said he just wanted to relax in the morning sun.

The water temperature was perfect and the waves invited us to do a little body surfing, which we did, blissfully unaware for the moment that we were being moved down the beach until Bruce called to us. When we saw him waving to us we also saw that a number of the construction workers were also waving at us.

"I'll bet they're wishing they could join us," I shouted to Jim.

"Let's head in; this surf is pretty rough," Jim shouted back.

We let a wave take us toward shore, then as our feet touched bottom we tried to wade ashore. That's when we discovered that we were caught in a serious undertow. Even though the water was only knee high, we were unable to get out of the water. The undertow swept us back into the surf. We kept trying to get in, but repeatedly got swept back. I lost my balance and was dragged under water by the undertow. I came up gasping, and Jim came over to help me.

Together we tried to make it to shore and together we got swept back out, now moving fairly rapidly down the beach into deeper water. We called to Bruce to help us. Being fresh, he quickly got to where we were, but when it became clear that he couldn't help us, we told him to go back in and save himself. Smaller and lighter than either Jim or myself, and still fresh, he was able to get back, and shouted that he would get help.

At some point I realized that help would probably be too late, and basically I gave up and waited to drown. I could no longer hear or see Jim, and assumed that he had already drowned.

I don't know how much time had passed; I vaguely remember a sense of anger at myself and wondering how our families would find out.

Then I was on the beach, and someone was pounding on my back, and I was coughing and gasping for air.

"Spit the water out, Dick," Bruce was shouting at me.

Gasping, choking, and desperate for air, I slowly became more aware of what was going on. Jim was on his knees close by, vomiting seawater, and looking pretty green. But at least he was on his knees.

Brown ankles and feet surrounded me, and Spanish from all around me was competing with Bruce's encouragement. I looked at Bruce and saw a smile begin on his face, as he realized that both of us were going to be OK.

We later pieced together the story of our dramatic rescue. When Bruce swam back in, after being unable to help either of us, he motioned to the construction workers to come over; some were already on their way. Later we learned that when they were waving to us they were actually trying to warn us that we were in danger.

Bruce must have said "muchas gracias" a hundred times—which was about the extent of the grasp of Spanish any of us had. One of the workers took Bruce over to the sign that read PELIGRO, and made clear to Bruce that this meant danger.

Another lesson in life—when you travel in a country where English isn't spoken, make sure you recognize and understand basic warning signs!

It was a very close call, and for me it was actually the second time I had been saved from drowning. The first time was when I was about ten. Sitting on the beach in Mazatlan, recovering from this latest incident, brought back memories and the emotions of the first incident very vividly, when I fell into a slate quarry on our farm without knowing how to swim. Luckily, quick-thinking playmates got a tree branch out to me, and as I was going down for the third time I managed to grab it and they pulled me to safety. So, it's understandable that to this day swimming is something I am not comfortable doing. The fact that I am unable to float makes the activity even more frightening to me. In fact, the most difficult part of flight school for me, when I was in training to become a pilot in the Marine Corps, was passing the swimming requirement. I seriously doubted that I could do it. If you ever saw the movie *An Officer and a Gentleman*, you may recall the horror experienced by one of the flight students when he had to escape from the "Dempsey Dumpster" in the pool, and was unable to. After he was rescued, he was dropped from the program and committed suicide because of his failure. When I saw the movie I had chills watching that scene of him in the pool; I knew exactly what he was feeling. I've never lost that feeling; it's always there, lurking in the back of my mind when I'm swimming.

The rest of our trip through Mexico, including the several days in Mexico City, was relatively uneventful. The most memorable activities were visiting the Chapultepec Castle in Mexico City, where US Marines earned the opening line in the Marine Corps Hymn ("...from the Halls of Montezuma...") and the restaurant in downtown Mexico City where Diego Rivera earned his supper by adorning the walls with a couple of his famous murals.

In Corpus Christi we turned the car over to two upperclassmen from the UW who drove it to Quantico, Virginia, where they were going to start their eight weeks of hell in the summer program for midshipmen (between the junior and senior years of college) who had selected the Marine Corps option. The Corpus Christi portion of our summer program was an orientation to Naval Air. We had familiarization flights on the remaining Navy flying boats, but the thrill of the four weeks was a ride in a Navy jet, sitting in the back seat. Some pilots turned the stick over to their backseat passengers, while others merely tried to make them as sick as quickly as possible so they could land and head for the Officers' Club. I got a little stick time, and then a little more sick time, as my pilot really wrung it out, in a series of tight, aerial maneuvers that had my stomach hiding behind the laces in my boots. Fortunately, I only turned a pale shade of green, and didn't heave my cookies. He was impressed.

At the end of our four weeks in Corpus Christi, we were airlifted to Little Creek, Virginia, for an orientation to the Marine Corps. The main day-time activity was learning about amphibious landings by actually doing them on the sandy beaches that were part of the Naval Station. The main evening activity was joining "choir practice" at the Officers' Club. There we learned to sing raunchy songs, hold our alcohol and flirt with the wives of officers who had shipped out for a cruise—all the things that constitute the finer points of becoming an officer and a gentleman.

Throughout the eight weeks, we were organized into a battalion of midshipmen from the different universities. The battalion consisted of several companies, with each company having several platoons and each platoon several squads. The companies and platoons competed against one another in various activities, from athletics to inspections to drills. As individuals, we rotated through a range of positions, from squad leader to battalion commander (for a lucky few). All the while we were being observed, to determine leadership potential and general suitability for the role of an officer in the US Navy or Marine Corps, and at the end of the summer these observations were sent back to the NROTC Commanders. I was fortunate that my company had an unusual number of outstanding middies, and we were always at the top of the competition. That resulted in a few of us being selected for the top leadership roles for a week, and I was lucky to be selected for one of the top roles. My main competition, on an individual level, was a wonderful guy from Kansas—an All-American football player. Kansas had several truly outstanding midshipmen in the Class of 1960, and they brought out the best in those of us who tried to keep up with them. The competition between us started in Corpus Christi, and extended to our liberty pursuits, including the "choir practice" in Little Creek, and ventures to Nuevo Laredo and Padre Island (where watermelons were four for a dollar) during our Texas segment. I lost track of the Kansas guys after the summer, but I remember fondly the thrill of the competition and the good times together.

My sophomore year at the UW brought major changes; our

independent, co-op houses closed and we moved into the brand new dormitories for men. Many of the older residents of Rofcre decided not to make the move. They had had enough of dormitory-style living in the military, so they moved into cheap apartments or some of the barely floating houseboats on Lake Union. For those of us who made the move, dorm life opened new opportunities and challenges. We lost a lot of the freedom and independence we had enjoyed in the relative anonymity of Greek Row. There would be no more Spring Ball orgies, no beer brewing in the basement. On the other hand, we were now part of a more visible voice of independent students on campus, and some of us, myself included, got involved in campus politics, through participation on the governing council of the Men's Dormitories. I was elected to the governing body on a platform of "open" visiting hours on Sunday. By "open" I meant that you could have a female guest in your room between noon and 4 p.m., as long as you kept the door open. When I contemplate the co-ed dorms now commonplace in colleges around the country, my quest (which I achieved) seems so quaint.

My junior year at the UW brought the most profound change in my personal life. You may recall that I mentioned earlier that Rofcre House had a basketball court where we also played volleyball, and often with some of the girls from the sorority across the alley joining in. I took an interest in one of the girls, and while she didn't reciprocate, since she was already going steady, she apparently saw enough potential in me to introduce me to her best friend, Dorene, a young woman who was working as a secretary in a shipping company in downtown Seattle. Dorene and I dated a few times during my freshman year, but nothing came of it, except for me getting my hands slapped a few times.

The next year Dorene went to Pacific Lutheran College, and we didn't see each other. However, in my junior year, I was becoming a more serious student, and needed someone to type term papers. I remembered that Dorene had excellent typing skills, and when I found that she was back in Seattle, had her own apartment in the "U District" and was attending night classes at the UW, I tracked her down. After making it clear that my interests were strictly business—I needed someone to type term papers and was willing to pay the going rate for this service—she agreed to meet me again.

One paper led to another, and another, and during that time she realized that I was no longer the wild thing she had dated almost two years earlier, and I realized that she was not the prude I thought she was. Soon, plates of homemade cookies awaited me when I brought my papers by for typing. That was followed by home-cooked meals, and when the Spring of 1959 rolled around, we realized that we were in love. Part of that love was grounded in lessons we had both learned while enduring unhappy home lives. We learned to be self-reliant, and to trust others who had made it through tough times. We knew that we wanted to raise a family in ways that we had not been able to enjoy.

At the start of my junior year I had decided to take the Marine Corps option in my NROTC commitment. That meant that in the summer of 1959 I would spend eight weeks in hell at Quantico, Virginia, a guest of the United States Marine Corps. Before I left for Quantico, Dorene and I went to see a popular movie playing that year—*Around the World in 80 Days*. As the movie came to an end, I proposed, saying that if she married me I promised I would show her the world. I don't think the promise made that much of an impact; she had already decided that a marriage between us, a Pennsylvania Dutchman and a Scandinavian maiden, was going to be an exciting challenge and a good thing. So, I left for Quantico with my feet ten feet off the ground.

My feet, and most other parts of my body, were quickly brought back down to earth during my first week by the Marine drill instructor who ran my platoon with all the rigor of boot camp and then some. The purpose of this eight-week program, carried out where newly commissioned Marine officers attend Basic School, was to see if you were fit, physically and psychologically, to be a Marine officer. Since they had eight weeks to make this determination, they went about this task in a manner as thorough as it was ruthless. Our first day there included the basic boot camp haircut and the issuing of uniforms and personal equipment, including a rifle which we would learn to disassemble, clean and reassemble in the dark before the eight weeks were over. Sometime during those first few days they took a close-up picture of each of us cleaning our rifle, and sent it to whomever we directed. My picture was sent to Dorene. I'm sure she wondered about the look in my eyes; it certainly wasn't the same love-filled softness she saw when I boarded the plane in Seattle a few days earlier. More like a "What the hell am I doing here?" look.

"The Proud. The Few. The Marines." I was quickly learning what that bit of advertising meant, and how they arrived at it. Basically, the Marine Corps operates on the assumption that every Marine, officer or enlisted, can be counted on without question to do what is called for in the heat of battle. Some have described the process of how they verify this assumption as one in which they tear you down and rebuild you in a way that meets Marine Corps' expectations. I wouldn't quarrel with that description. Certainly, by the end of the second week of boot camp, whether it is the eight-week program that I was experiencing or the boot camp that enlisted personnel experience, one was aware that your sense of self was being reshaped. While the opening gambit of this process had a heavy dose of fear, or at least intimidation, it was much more complex than that.

You learned that whatever limits you may have had, physically or emotionally, they can be stretched, and while there is pain in that process, it starts to feel good as you realize you can do better. You learned that teamwork really is at the heart of successful efforts, and that if you hold back from a total commitment to a team effort you'll probably pay a heavy price for it sooner or later. You learned the basics of what every person in a squad does, so that if and when you became a platoon leader you will have done everything you may be directing your troops to do, and they will know that you have been through it too.

At the centre of the eight-week program was a daily (sometimes twice daily) run of the Hill Trail—a brutal journey in the heat and humidity of July and August of several miles up and down Virginia hills with a full pack on your back, a steel helmet on your head and a rifle over your shoulder. By the third week I was cruising over the trail, and frequently carrying the rifle or the backpack of a suffering soul. That's when you begin to feel what it means, in a very small way, to experience the pride of being a Marine. You were meeting the hardest thing they were throwing at you and taking it in your stride. Now, in my 67th year, with part of a lung removed, borderline chronic heart failure and experiencing the extreme fatigue associated with chemotherapy, I often think of the exhilaration I felt at the end of the Hill Trail run, as I pull myself to the top of the 14th step to my study. God, what I would give to have one tenth of the energy and strength I had at the end of that summer!

By the end of the eight weeks there were considerably fewer of us than at the start of the program. Some left on their own—DOR (Drop On Request)—as they knew the Marine Corps was not for them. Some left because the Marine Corps decided they did not have the right stuff. In either case, they would go back to their NROTC unit and take the Naval Officer option during their senior year. I not only survived that summer, I excelled, and I believe that I did so because I had learned in the eight years of mental hardship I endured in our broken family that I could not be broken; that I had the psychological strength to endure the testing Quantico offered. And the hard, physical work I carried out as a farm boy, often covered with sweat and itching from the hay or straw chaff that stuck to your sweating body in the hot, humid summers of Eastern Pennsylvania had honed me for the physical challenges of Quantico.

I went back to Seattle at the end of this summer and moved into several leadership positions in the NROTC Battalion of midshipmen at the UW. I was chosen to represent the Navy ROTC when the three ROTC units on campus (Army, Air Force and Navy) sent a person to meet with the Governor and accept his annual Proclamation of Governor's Day on the University of Washington. On that day, the Governor came to the campus, reviewed a parade of all the ROTC units, and made a speech about honoring the UW when we became commissioned officers in a few weeks. For the seniors, it was the highlight of four years of early morning drills, military science courses, summer cruises and the knowledge that shortly they would have a single brass bar on the tip of each collar designating them as a Second Lieutenant or an Ensign. For the freshman, the parade and review was a pain in the ass—a miserable way to be spending a sunny spring day. They, and many of the upperclassmen, were thinking how they'd rather be over at Green Lake with a six-pack and a co-ed.

For a number of us in the NROTC Battalion, it meant that the end of a double life was approaching, and we would be able to exhale. As midshipmen on Navy scholarships we were held to many of the same regulations that applied to the middies at the US Naval Academy at Annapolis. One of these regulations specified that a midshipman was not to marry. Well, the reality was that about ten per cent of the senior midshipmen at the UW were already married, and most of them were in the top of the class. One, the best man in my December 1959 wedding (six months prior to graduation), even had two children. Another reality was that several of the officers/instructors in the NROTC unit were aware of this reality and chose to turn a blind eye—all but one. In the weeks before graduation there was rumor that he was collecting names and was going to turn us in. We could have been denied our commissions, and forced to repay the US Navy for four years of education. Needless to say, we were sweating blood. In the end, nothing happened. I suspect that there was a showdown in the boardroom, and that rationality prevailed. The problem was so big that if the Department of the Navy was informed, the situation would reflect far worse on the NROTC unit at the UW and the officers involved than it would on the individual cases of the married midshipmen.

So, on a sunny day in early June of 1960 I celebrated two singular events in the history of the Fehnel family. In the morning I put on the black graduation robe and received my baccalaureate degree (a BA, with a double major in Political Science and Far Eastern Affairs), the first male in our family to achieve this honor. In the afternoon I put on the starched, white dress uniform of a Second Lieutenant in the United States Marine Corps (Regular) and became the first male in the Fehnel family to achieve this rank. I accepted my Second Lieutenant bars with a proud, happy wife at my side (though neither of us was foolish enough to wear our wedding rings that afternoon). We put them on the next day, as we loaded our '54 Chevy for the drive across the country to Quantico, where I was to begin what I hoped was a career in the Marine Corps, and an opportunity to learn more lessons in life.

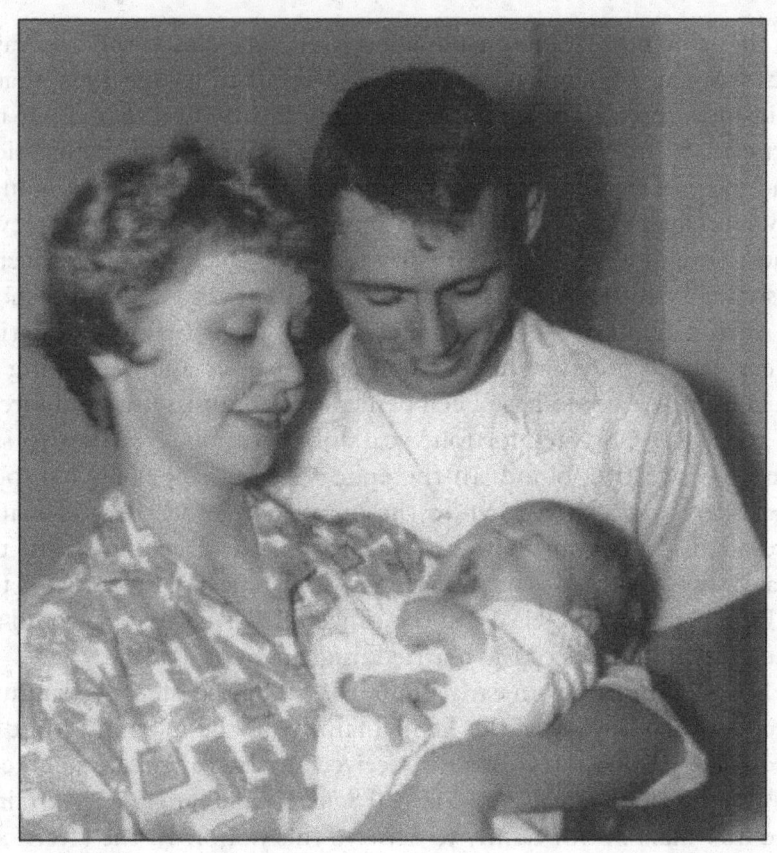

Milton, Florida. August 1961.
Deborah Susan joins the family.

CHAPTER 8
SEMPER FIDELIS

SURPRISINGLY, MY BIGGEST CHALLENGE, NEXT TO
PASSING THE ENDURANCE-SWIMMING REQUIREMENT,
WAS OVERCOMING MY FEAR OF ... HEIGHTS ...
I DEALT WITH IT AS I HAD LEARNED TO DEAL WITH
OTHER NEGATIVE ISSUES IN MY LIFE;
I SEALED IT OFF IN A COMPARTMENT OF MY MIND
AND FOCUSED LIKE HELL ON WHAT I HAD TO DO.

The only money I ever borrowed from a family member was $400 from my Aunt Omegene, which I used to buy my Marine Corps uniform and the sword all Marine officers are required to have. Paying it back on a Second Lieutenant's salary of $222.81 a month in 1960 took some time, but it was done as promised. A lesson learned from my grandfather: "Always ... always pay back what you owe as quickly as you can." Regrettably, I got rid of the uniforms a few years ago, but the sword hangs over the doorway leading from my office, a reminder of my brief but rewarding career in the Corps.

My career started with the prescribed tour of duty in the Marine Corps Basic Officer School in Quantico, Virginia. Here the traditions, the skills, the *espirit* of the Corps are learned and relearned and practised until they become second nature. The highlights of Basic School included the week-long field exercise that concluded our training—a bitterly cold and damp week in the wintry month of January. Another highlight was the celebration of the Marine Corps Birthday Ball on November 13. The Marine Corps traces its history back to November 13, 1775, and its birthday celebration is the social highlight of the year for all Marines. It is celebrated worldwide, even in the tiniest outpost. Since Marines guard all US Embassies and all US Naval ships, wherever you are in the world, the chances are you can find a party on November 13. I was in Pakistan once, long after I had left active duty. My host for the consulting work I was doing for USAID discovered that I was a former Marine officer. Since we shared that background, when November 13 rolled around I found myself seated at the table of honor, between him and the Director of USAID/Pakistan, who was also a former Marine.

But none of the Marine birthday parties I ever attended compared to my first one during basic school in 1960. The toasts were many and the champagne flowed freely, perhaps too freely as events proved. One of the decorated Marine captains, who was an instructor in Basic School and had earned his decorations in Korea, almost lost his right eye when it was hit by a champagne cork. The Ball was held in the dining-room of the BOQ (Bachelor Officers' Quarters) and at some point late in the evening several of the bachelor officers decided to take their dates upstairs to their quarters. Their idea of foreplay was to instruct their dates on how to march, stark naked except for high heels, in the hallway outside their rooms. That bit of close-order drill became part of the legend of Basic Class E-1960. And speaking of legends, the Commanding Officer of basic school during my time there was none other than the legendary Louis Wilson, one of the most highly decorated Marines during the Korean conflict. He had earned a chest full of medals, but he only ever wore one—the US Medal of Honor. He later became the Commandant of the Marine Corps. That night, as I introduced my wife to him in the official reception line, I trembled as I stood before him. He stood about 6' 3", weighed about 200 pounds, and had a handsome face worthy of chiseling onto Mount Rushmore.

During the last week of basic school you find out where your first real tour of duty will take you. I had applied for flight school, in Pensacola, Florida and was thrilled to be sent there. So, in late January, 1961, Dorene and I packed the Chevy again, and said goodbye to the little cottage we had rented on the north bank of the Rappahannock River, across from the city of Fredericksburg, Virginia, on the very grounds where the Union Army had encamped a hundred years earlier.

In 1961 Pensacola, Florida, was culturally and politically southern Alabama. The Sears & Roebuck store was still segregated. It was the first time I had seen signs on drinking fountains and bathrooms that said "Whites Only". George Wallace began one of his many successful runs for Governor of Alabama that year, and we heard lots of the racist campaign rhetoric in the panhandle of Florida.

The US Navy flight school was only slightly less segregated at that time than the civilian world that surrounded it. There were no black Marine officers and only one or two black Navy officers in flight training. I don't recall that any of the many flight instructors were black. But as the rigors of flight training bore down on me I became less concerned about the skin of others, and worried only about saving my own.

I had opted for flight school for several reasons. Firstly, my father had flown during the barnstorming days of the 1920s. He had been living in Chicago at that time, and flew out of the same field that Amelia Earhart occasionally flew from. It was a field used by many of the pilots, male and female, that flew in the pylon races so popular in those days. A treasured family photo is of my dad and Amelia standing next to a plane on that Chicago airfield. During the happier days on the farm, when my mother was still alive, we heard many tales about their days in Chicago, and about the thrills of flying. So I jumped at the chance to learn how to fly. Besides, flying seemed a damn sight better than marching, the other primary alternative a Marine officer had, unless you wanted to consider riding around in a tank, which had absolutely no appeal to me.

Surprisingly, my biggest challenge, next to passing the endurance-swimming requirement, was overcoming my fear of flying—or more precisely, my fear of heights. For some reason, I had never been really aware of how fearful I was of heights until I began to peer over the side of the small two-seater the Navy used in flight training. What an inopportune time to become aware of this condition! I dealt with it as I had learned to deal with other negative issues in my life; I sealed it off in a compartment of my mind and focused like hell on what I had to do. But when the flight sessions were over, the demons were let loose. Many days I rode home from flight school stretched out in the back seat of the car, nauseous from the migraine headache that was busting through that compartment door.

When my day to fly solo came around, Lieutenant Morgan, my flight instructor, hopped out of the back seat during a short stop, slapped the side of the plane and said, "You're ready; take her up there. I'll see you when you get down. Good luck!"

I hardly remember a thing about that solo flight. I'm sure I never banked the plane more than ten degrees, and probably made the widest approach to Saufly Field, our training field, ever recorded. The Navy must have liked to stick its finger in the eye of Fate, because you made your solo on your 13th flight if your instructor thought you were ready. My flight log shows I was ready on June 27, 1961, and I piloted that little T-34 around Saufly (along with about five hundred other student pilots and their instructors) for 1.3 hours and made six touch-and-go landings. I only remember the last one, when I was able to taxi to my parking spot and gratefully turn the engine off. I had survived.

Next stop in flight school was Whiting Field, located outside Milton, Florida, about fifteen miles east of Pensacola. Whiting became our home for the rest of flight school. It had housing for married officers, and Dorene and I nestled down in one of the newly remodeled ranch houses and prepared for the birth of our first child. Being pregnant in Florida throughout the summer is as miserable as you can imagine, but Dorene endured, even without air-conditioning. Relief came on August 31, when Deborah Susan Fehnel was born in the Milton Community Hospital. I was allowed to stand in the doorway and watch the birth, while Dorene slept through it, under the influence of twilight medication. Our lives changed that night, as all new parents come to realize. It was a change we welcomed, and now that it had arrived we settled into our respective routines.

For me, that meant flying and more flying. At Whiting Field we trained in T-28s, single engine, propeller-driven attack planes from World War II and Korea. The T-28 was a powerful plane, and could be unforgiving, unlike the kittenish T-34s we had flown before then. More than one student pilot "bought the farm" trying to master the T-28, and I had at least two very close calls. But I persisted, and flew through the curriculum of ground school, the academic side of training, as well as the flying part of training, which was now getting more interesting. We learned basic air-to-air combat skills, firing live ammo at a drone during strafing runs; we learned formation flying, which I enjoyed immensely because it allowed me to show off the smooth hand-eye co-ordination I had learned driving a tractor around the farm, hooking up to various pieces of farm equipment, which required great precision. And we learned basic navigation skills, including night flying, which scared the hell out of me at first.

But the high-point of flying the T-28 was "care-quals"—qualifying in landing and taking off from an aircraft carrier. As I look back over my brief flying career, qualifying stands out as the most thrilling and satisfying day of all. Everything came together for me on March 3, 1962. I led my flight of four planes into the Gulf of Mexico, where we rendezvoused with the USS Antietam (CV-36). I made eight perfect approaches and landings on the pitching deck of the carrier, and then circled while the other planes in my flight finished their qualification runs. Unlike my solo flight, when I was scared out of my wits and couldn't remember much of that day except the smell of fear in the cockpit, I remember my day of qualifying on an aircraft carrier in great detail and with considerable pride. On that day I was at the top of my game in a T-28.

It was also my last flight in this aircraft; immediately after qualifying we started flying the SNB, the Navy's small twin-engine aircraft. This was a slow, plodding plane used as a scout because it could stay aloft for long periods of time, and then as a trainer, primarily for cross-country navigation in the US Navy flight command. Because it had a tail wheel, it was a tricky plane to land, especially at night and in a crosswind. Landing it frustrated many a pilot, including my instructor, who couldn't believe how easily I learned to land this baby.

The highlight of this phase of training was for an instructor and two student pilots to plan and execute a cross-country trip, demonstrating our skills at navigation. I chose to fly to Allentown-Bethlehem-Easton Airport, my hometown airport. This suited the other student, who was from Buffalo, New York. So we planned a trip from Milton, Florida, to ABE, then on to Floyd Bennett Naval Air Station on Long Island where we would stay overnight, then on to Buffalo and back to Florida. I had told my sister when we would be landing at ABE, and after the landing the tower instructed me to taxi to the main terminal to pick up a passenger. This seemed rather odd; I explained that this was a Navy plane and we weren't authorized to carry passengers. The tower insisted, so I complied. As I pulled into the temporary parking spot, the "passenger" appeared; it was my father, walking about ten feet off the ground, buoyed by paternal pride. The crew chief opened the door, my dad climbed aboard, was given a set of headphones, and we taxied to another parking spot where we shut down and took an hour break, when every relative in my family came by to have a picture taken with me next to the plane.

Obviously, my sister had called my father, and every other living relative in the vicinity, to come to the airport and greet the briefly returning warrior son, brother, nephew and cousin. Though my father and I remained at odds, it didn't prevent us from keeping in touch on my visits back to the Lehigh Valley. So, I wasn't surprised to see him there, but I never did hear the story of how he talked the ground controller into being a part of his little dramatic surprise. In today's post-9/11 environment that would never happen.

I was again piloting when we took off, and wagged the tail of the aircraft as we flew over the field, to the displeasure of the instructor. Feeling pretty cocky, we flew into the New York City area, where the incredible volume of air traffic and rapid-fire landing pattern instructions issued by the air traffic controller handling our plane soon shattered my cockiness. In the Navy Training Command we had been taught to repeat the commands given by the air traffic controller, to insure that we had copied them down on our knee-pad correctly. I began to read the instructions back when the controller interrupted me and said he didn't have time to listen to them. Floyd Bennett Naval Air Station is tucked into a bay on Long Island between JFK and LaGuardia. Our approach from ABE took us past Newark Airport, and in a matter of seconds I realized that I was over my head, in terms of trying to keep abreast of all the instructions being communicated to all the aircraft in the landing patterns of the four fields. Fortunately, our instructor and the other student pilot had copied down our instructions and read them to me as we threaded our way into Floyd Bennett NAS. I was as relieved to land as I had been when I solo-ed!

When we returned to Milton and Whiting Field, I immediately began the next phase of flight training—flying helicopters. I had made the choice for helicopters because I didn't think I was ready for jets. Unfortunately, some of my contemporaries allowed testosterone to make the decision for them, and they died wrestling a type of plane they weren't ready to fly.

In reality, flying helicopters in the 1960s was much more difficult than just about any other type of aircraft because they didn't have autopilot or power-boost systems yet. Basically, a helicopter is unstable, with the aerodynamics of a rock; unlike fixed-wing aircraft, which glide if your engine stops. When you were flying a helicopter in those days, your hands and feet were each doing something different, so co-ordination was essential to a smooth flight. I had very good co-ordination and breezed through the last few months of flight school with little difficulty, qualifying first in the little two-passenger Bell and then in the larger Sikorsky HSS-1, which at that time was the main type of helicopter used by the Marine Corps for combat operations as it could carry a squad of combat-ready troops.

On July 25, 1962 I earned my wings, a fully qualified Marine pilot ready to take my place in the Fleet Marine Force. I was assigned to the 2nd Marine Air Wing at New River, North Carolina, so Dorene and I packed up again (by now the '54 Chevy was history, and we were driving a new VW Microbus) and headed for Jacksonville, North Carolina, to set up home. We found a two-bedroom house, off base but in the middle of the Marine community. Little did I realize when we moved in that I would be spending less than a month sleeping in that house.

Shortly after I joined my squadron, we were sent urgently on an all-night flight to Oxford, Mississippi, where we joined the US Army and National Guard troops ordered by President Kennedy to assist in the integration of James Meredith at the University of Mississippi. So, my first taste of real military maneuvers was putting down a domestic disturbance, not flying off to some foreign soil. Actually, this was an important test for America, and in some respects, even more so for the Marine Corps. At that time, many Marine Officers were good ol' Southern boys. So here was their first test of values. Would they accept the orders as given even though they felt strongly that James Meredith should seek a college education somewhere else, preferably in the North, or would they find ways to diminish our presence—such as finding mechanical difficulties with their aircraft, grounding them for a day or more.

Our job was to fly Army and National Guard troops to strategic locations around Oxford where they set up roadblocks to prevent locals from coming into the campus and taking over. We did this primarily at night to hide our maneuvers and to minimize becoming targets for the locals to shoot at. It was a tense situation and several of the Marine helicopters did report being fired on by locals.

My worst incident was when one of the Army grunts left a surprise in the plane when he and his buddies jumped out—a discharging tear gas grenade. Our quick-thinking crew chief kicked it out the door as we lifted off, but the climb out was a little dicey being partially blinded and flying in the dark, with other choppers all around us.

We had some heated debates in the dormitory we were housed in, but they were brief and our Commanding Officer made sure that every man knew his role and carried it out. Soon the only debate was whether the Yankees or the Cardinals would win the World

Series. Watching TV was the only entertainment we had because we certainly weren't welcome in town.

Before our tour in Mississippi came to an end I was evacuated back to Jacksonville. Dorene was hospitalized, having suffered a miscarriage. So for a few days we were together, and I was able to try my hand at my other role in life, being a father to our one-year-old daughter while Mommy rested in the hospital.

But again, political events intervened, and the whole Marine Air Wing was moving to Mayport, Florida, where we became part of the blockade of Cuba during the Cuban Missile Crisis. The new home of the squadron became the carrier USS Okinawa (LPH-3), and for the next two months we spent most of our time at sea, in the warm waters of the Caribbean, or on rotation to the Naval base at Mayport where we could take on provisions and run landing exercises on Florida beaches.

Much has been written about the geopolitics of the Cuban Missile Crisis, and there is little I can add except a few tales of what it was like from the point of view of a rather lowly Marine helicopter pilot participating in the blockade. It also helps to know that my secondary MOS (military occupation specialty) was that of an intelligence officer, so I served as our squadron's intelligence S-2, the designation given for this role. It was actually in that capacity that my most memorable moments of this campaign occurred.

It was generally accepted that the blockade was the first move in a grand chess game, and that the only way the United States was going to insure that the Russian missiles were removed was to invade and seize the missile sites. With that in mind, we spent all of our time when we were in Mayport practicing landings, and all of our time at sea keeping watch for Russian vessels bringing more missiles.

During the practice landings the brains of the Marine Corps came to realize that the current methods of off-loading several battalions of Marines from aircraft carriers and other troop-carrying ships was horribly outmoded and inefficient. In essence we weren't using helicopters for a vertical assault, we were using them like landing ships used by Marines in the island-hopping battles of World War II, in effect a horizontal assault. That realization sparked an incredible period of innovation. For several days all the intelligence officers, operations officers and commanding officers gathered in a huge auditorium on the Naval Base and literally generated a whole new philosophy, strategy and operation method for conducting a vertical assault, using the maneuverability of helicopters in a way that maximized their capability. What came out of that flash of inspiration and innovation became the backbone of US Marine tactics for vertical assaults that may still be in use today. I was like the proverbial fly on the wall, present as the brainstorming and debating picked up energy and as generals, colonels, majors and a few captains moved toy ships and planes about on a big map, and sketched movements on an overhead projector. It was a very exciting process; from the way the senior officers were carrying on, I knew I was witnessing something transcendent in the history of the Marine Corps.

Once we worked out the new strategy on paper, we then put it into practice. Errors were corrected, and in a few days we were ready to try it in combat, should the need arise.

Back out on the blockade, I was part of an incident that my family loves to hear about, even for the tenth or twentieth time. While on blockade, we flew search missions looking for Russian ships. One day while we were searching our designated quadrant, the Okinawa's Communication Center contacted us and said they had just received an alert from the long-range search planes that a possible bogey (Russian tanker) was entering our zone. They gave us coordinates for the target and we cranked the RPMs up and headed toward the spot in the Caribbean. I should mention, for the sake of this story, that in those days I had a reputation for pretty remarkable eyesight. I could see things before they became discernible to others. So, my eyes were scanning the horizon as we zoomed along, and sure enough there on the horizon I picked out a large tanker, like the kind the Russians were using to ship missiles to Cuba. I could see the faint shape of a Red Star on the smokestack, so we radioed back to the Okinawa that we were going in for a closer look and possible verification.

Suddenly, after several hours of boredom, our pulses were racing as we put the chopper just above water and headed for the ship at top speed. We told the crew chief, in the belly of the chopper, to get his rifle ready in case we were fired at, and I loosened up the

Dick on the farm.
Summer 1940.

Dick and his younger brother, Roger,
on the farm. Date unknown.

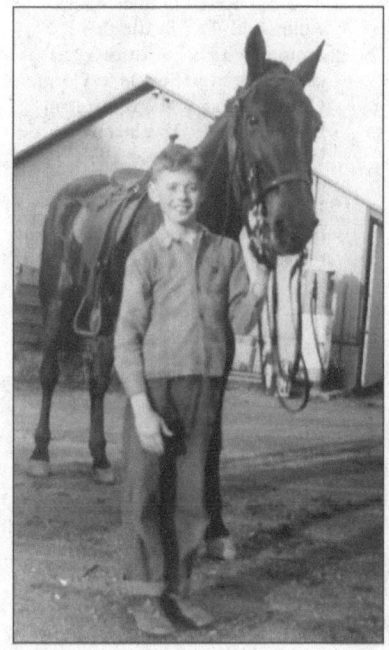

Dick with his horse, Mickey.

Dick as a teenager.
Date unknown.

Above: Dressed in midshipman whites with VW Beatle that transported Dick with two classmates from Seattle to Corpus Christi, Texas, and a return trip from Quantico, Virginia to Seattle via this stop in Penna. 1958.

Left: Traditional midshipman dunking in Frosh Pond, University of Washington. May 1958.

Dick with his sister, Lina. Lina organized a family welcome when Dick flew in to his hometown airport. 1962.

1/Lt Richard A Fehnel, USMC, receiving his wings. July 1962.

Left: Bringing Douglas Martin "home". May 1968.

Below: Playtime with Doug. Bethesda, Maryland. 1970.

Right: Dick receives a teaching award at the University of Oregon from Dean Kelly. June 1977.

Below: Non-traditional professor, Walden University. Summer 1982.

Left: Experiencing Bangladesh. 1984.

Below: With Dara – the joys of grandparenthood. Summer 1987.

Above: Midlands Partnership/National Programme launch. April 1997.

Below: Women's Higher Education Conference, Durban. 1999.

Above: Dinner with Nico Cloete, CHET. 2002.

Below: "Forever" friends in the Wallowa Mountains, Oregon. From left to right: Judy Maas (who set up the blind date in 1957), Rosemary and Walt Ellis, and Dick. Summer 2004.

holster of the .45 on my hip. We came at the ship at an angle that caught the glare on the sun on the smokestack, so we couldn't see anything clearly. Then, just as we approached the side of the ship, my flying partner who was on the controls, honked back on the stick and the chopper popped up next to the ship, giving me a clear view of the word Texaco, just beneath the big red star. My moment of glory made the rounds on the Okinawa, as we sheepishly reported what we found, and by the time we landed back aboard ship someone had scrawled on the blackboard in the ready room that 1st/Lt Fehnel had made the best sighting of potential enemy combatants of the day.

In a way, it was very useful humor. It helped to break the tension that gripped our ship, as well as the world. A few days later we went back to Mayport, and our ship was docked along with others on patrol. At some point on our last day ashore, I was dispatched to the Fleet Command ship, berthed at another dock about a twenty-minute walk away. I was told to come armed. When I got there and reported to the duty officer I found out why. I was given a brief case that was cuffed to my left wrist, and the key carefully stowed in my pocket. I had just been given the Cuba invasion plans for our squadron and the Marine infantrymen stationed on the Okinawa.

I remember walking back to my ship, and reaching a juncture in the docks. I stopped and looked down into the waters and wondered what would happen if I unlocked the briefcase and dumped the invasion plans into the bay. Then the gruff, deep voice of my platoon commander at basic school rang through my head: "They'll throw you so deep in the brig, they'll have to shoot beans in for you to eat."

He was right, of course. I don't even know why I had that thought. I guess I was confronting the reality of real war, and didn't like the prospects. I liked them even less when I got to our ship and turned the document over to Colonel Bianchi, our CO. Together with the Operations Officer we studied the plan and the map. I would have to brief the pilots of our squadron on some of the top secret plan's details. It was very grim stuff. Our squadron was going to be flying the Marines on the Okinawa right into the heart of the missile base that our U-2s had identified. The expected casualty rate for the choppers was fifty per cent on the first wave. I felt sick.

All the ships in Mayport hoisted anchor that night and we headed for a spot in the ocean from which we would launch the invasion of Cuba. It is a tradition in the US Navy that every night before "lights out", the ship's Chaplain says a prayer. The prayer on the night of October 28 was one I will never forget. I don't remember the words the Chaplain used; I remember the passion. It was a long prayer, but the entire ship was completely silent. A few young men silently wept, fearing tomorrow would be their last day on earth; others were writing letters to be passed on by a member of the ship's crew. I lay in my bunk thinking about Dorene and Debbie, and the fifty per cent casualty rate on the first wave. When the Chaplain ended his prayer there was a hitch in his voice. He knew.

And then morning came and with it salvation! Overnight, Khrushchev had blinked. The moment passed, but we stayed on the blockade until the end of November, just in case the Russian Bear changed his mind.

My last flight was on December 2, 1962, when we off-loaded all the squadron gear from the Okinawa to our old quarters at New River. On December 3 I checked into the US Naval Hospital at Camp Lejeune, the huge Marine Base next to the New River facility.

For months a growing pain had bothered me, first in my right testicle, then in the groin area. The flight surgeon aboard ship diagnosed it as a blocked semen duct and had me sit in hot baths. Some days the pain was too much to fly. So, as soon as we were done off-loading I went to the hospital for a further examination, under sedation. When I woke up, Dorene was sitting by my bed and had obviously been crying. I became aware of surgical dressings around my testicles and a throbbing pain in that area. Soon a doctor appeared and he sat on a corner of the bed and told me what they had done. First they did a biopsy on the right testicle, which revealed a malignancy. Then they removed the right testicle. There was some suspicion that the malignancy may have spread into the lymph nodes, so they were sending me to the US Naval Hospital at Bethesda, Maryland. I didn't realize it at the time, but my flying career had just been permanently grounded.

Chapter 9
Cancer Round One

I CRIED AGAIN, THIS TIME TEARS OF JOY.
BUT I HAD LEARNED ANOTHER LESSON—NOT TO LET
MY OPTIMISM CAUSE ME TO DROP MY GUARD.

New River Air Facility, North Carolina. April, 1963.
Last flight before being medically retired.

The flashing red lights told me I was in an ambulance even though the siren was silent.

"Where are we?" I asked the Navy corpsman by my side.

"Between Anacostia and Bethesda. How are you doing?"

"OK."

I remembered being taken from the hospital at Camp Lejeune on a gurney, but then the sedative must have kicked in and I couldn't remember anything about the flight from North Carolina to Washington, DC.

It was night and a gentle rain was falling, giving the ambulance ride an artificial sense of serenity. Anacostia is a Naval Air Station in south-eastern Washington, DC. We were headed north-west, across the city to the massive Naval Hospital in suburban Bethesda, Maryland. As we approached the hospital its single granite tower loomed high over the surrounding neighborhood, bathed in spotlights and glistening in the rain. Christmas decorations in the windows of colonial style houses near the hospital sparkled, their images refracted and multiplied by the raindrops on the windows of the ambulance. Several of the tall pine trees at the front of the hospital were decorated with Christmas lights. Somehow, I wasn't in a Christmas spirit. Being told you have cancer takes the edge off a festive mood. It was December 18, 1962, the eve of our third wedding anniversary.

A room and bed were waiting for me in the urology ward, on the 13th floor of the tower. (Once again the Navy said, "Screw you" to superstitions; have you ever been on the 13th floor of a building in the USA?) I had never been to USNH Bethesda before, and only knew of it from media reports, vaguely remembering when James Forrestal, America's first Secretary of Defense, committed suicide by leaping from the 16th floor of the tower. Some Marine and Navy pilots I had met in flight school had spent time there recovering from Korean war wounds and they also talked about the hospital, some with affection, others not. Like all military hospitals of that time, the walls were pastel green, hallways were polished and waxed, causing every step taken in a leather-soled shoe to squeak. Those were the days before the ubiquitous crepe-soled shoes or sneakers became standard wear of all hospital ward personnel.

A nurse checked me in and made me as comfortable as is possible when your scrotum is wrapped in surgical gauze and you have a deep ache where your right testicle used to be. The Navy Commander with whom I shared the room greeted me kindly. He turned out to be a real advocate for me when, after a day and a half of not being told about my diagnosis and treatment plan, he pulled rank and shouted at the Navy doctors to tell me what the hell was going on. These were the old days when doctors communicated little with patients, before any notion of patient rights. Furthermore, being treated by doctors who were at least one or two ranks higher than me further diminished any obligation to share information with me.

By then Dorene had joined me. She and our daughter Debbie had been driven by two Marines from Jacksonville to Bethesda to be at my side—an all night drive. It was a time of great turmoil for them, and to this day Dorene can't remember where they stayed that first week in Bethesda.

I was told that I had a mixed form of testicular cancer (dysgerminoma and embryoma), fairly common among young men my age. The particular mix I had made prognosis difficult, since one form did not respond well to treatment, while the other did. After further review it was decided that I would be treated through a combination of further surgery to remove any lymph glands that might have metastasized, followed by deep radiation therapy. They made it sound fairly routine. The surgery was scheduled for mid-January, so in the spirit of the season, I was allowed to spend Christmas away from the hospital. After another week of recovery from the first operation, we headed for my sister's home, just south of Bethlehem, Pennsylvania.

I had grown up in a farmhouse from whose southern facing windows we could see the star of Bethlehem from a distance of twelve miles during the Christmas season. I spent hours watching it twinkle mysteriously in the cold winter nights before drifting off to sleep. It was the main Christmas attraction for the City of Bethlehem, but I had never seen it as close as it would be when we were at my sister's house—less than a mile from the star. Would it shine on our little family and give us hope, as the original Star of Bethlehem did for other travellers?

What is it about the human spirit that allows us to put faith in man-made representations of something more metaphysical? As I looked at the Star of Bethlehem from up close I could see the rusting steel structure on which it was hung; several of the light bulbs were out, giving it a somewhat used look. Pushed by the diagnosis of cancer to the edge of my beliefs, I now found doubts about faith. I had come to believe primarily in myself, and in whatever tools helped me achieve my goals. These goals may have started as dreams, but they were soon converted into practical goals, achieved through hard work. I believed in the mechanical principles that kept my planes flying, not some mystical notion of God as my co-pilot. I believed in the hard cold steel of the rifle on my shoulder or the .45 on my hip and my ability to make them do as I wished, not with any notion of divine retribution if forced to use them. In the months ahead I would be forced to face my ambivalence about faith in a God that had taken my mother at the age of thirty-seven, had put a woman in our family who destroyed it and now made me fight for my life.

Our family is like a lot of families; we don't talk about the elephant that is sitting in the middle of the living-room. It's as if refusing to recognize and discuss an issue will make it disappear, or at least diminish its impact. So that Christmas we pretended that life was normal—a pretense that gave way when we went to bed and Dorene and I held tightly to each other, each silently fearing that this might be our last Christmas together, just as we have been doing this last week, as Christmas 2005 has come around.

At the end of the first week in January we returned to Bethesda, and turned our attention to finding a place where Dorene and Debbie could live during my hospitalization. As if to challenge my ambivalence in faith, we appealed to the Minister of a Lutheran Church in Bethesda, and parishioners Evie and Julian Streng responded by opening their home to us for as long as we needed. Evie worked in the Defense Department and Julian was a salesman at a Ford dealer in Bethesda. They had met and married late in life (they were both in their fifties when we met them), so Dorene and Debbie were treated as lovingly as if they were a daughter and granddaughter. Their kindness and flexibility was a blessing we never forgot.

On January 16, 1962, I underwent surgery—a bilateral transabdominal retroperitoneal lymphadenectomy. The actual surgery was worse than its name. Six surgeons, working in teams of two over a nine-hour period carried out the bloody operation. Basically, the procedure is to open you up "from stem to sternum", take all your insides out and keep them bathed in a solution, while the surgeons then carefully root around looking for lymph glands and snipping them out. Since most of these glands lie along the spine, the snipping has to be done with extreme caution. One wrong snip and you bleed to death on the table; another wrong snip and you're paralyzed for life; another wrong snip and you're impotent. Ironically, one of the six surgeons who operated on me that day was diagnosed with the same disease a little while later. He chose to forego the surgery and went straight into radiation treatment. I don't think he made it.

Of the sixty lymph glands removed from me, eighteen had already metastasized. When I found that out weeks later, I began to curse the flight surgeon who had misdiagnosed my case, but realized my anger wasn't going to change anything.

Forty-two years after that operation I can still remember the extreme pain I suffered when I began to regain consciousness, several days after the surgery. I have never felt pain like that. Demerol would take the edge off the pain for a while, and allow me to sleep, but there's only so much of that good stuff that you should take. The sutures that held me together seemed so fragile; in fact several popped and had to be re-sewn. I was afraid that with any sudden move or a cough or sneeze my guts would come spilling out. I had been moved to a private room; I probably would have driven a roommate crazy by my constant moaning in pain, of which I was largely unaware. My earliest recollection of post-operative recovery is being in a darkened room, with a nurse hovering over me, silhouetted against the dim night-time lights of the hallway, forcing me to sit on the edge of the bed and telling me to cough so I wouldn't get pneumonia. The next memory is of the smell of coffee, which made me want to puke. It was months until I could stand the smell of what had been a staple drink in my life as a pilot.

It took weeks before I had the courage to stand up reasonably straight, enduring the pain that simple action brought on. It was also weeks since I had had a cigarette, so I credit the operation for doing what I had been unable to do on my own after only a few years of light smoking.

In late January I began radiation therapy. When described to you in the comfort of your hospital room or a doctor's office, it sounds benign. In reality, it was as scary and weird as a horror movie. The nuclear medicine program was housed in an underground facility accessible through a long, spooky walk through a tunnel that connected it to the main hospital. The patients who were in the waiting room were a shock to me; they all looked terminally ill. I immediately imagined myself looking like that after treatment had begun and wondered whether this was the best way to proceed.

Then it was my turn to enter the treatment chamber. It was a cold, impersonal room, totally lacking in any sort of human quality. I was placed on a slab, and then this monstrous machine moved menacingly over me. On the first visit the radiologist determined the areas of my body that were to be treated and small, permanent tattoos were inked into my skin. They are still there. They provided the boundary makers or reference points so that in all future treatments the machine would irradiate the exact same areas.

When I was properly lined up, everyone left the chamber, and the huge lead-lined door closed ominously. The mere sound of its heavy closing underscored the isolation I felt. Then the machine started coming to life, the whirling sound gaining in pitch and loudness like the Ride of the Valkyries. A mechanical voice sternly reminded me not to move, and I wanted to get up and run!

After several minutes the Valkyries rode away, the door latches released, the door opened and the radiologist, now beginning to look like young Dr Frankenstein in my twisted mind, came in and turned me over and positioned me for a second treatment. The same chilling procedure ensued. He retreated to safety through the lead door; the door swung shut and the latches clicked in place. A minute or so of silence and then the monster started moaning again, and the voice said, "Don't move" and the Valkyries did their thing.

Over the next ten weeks I went through eighty-eight such sessions, receiving a lifetime's worth of radiation. On one of my early journeys through the tunnel I discovered a little chapel about midway between the main hospital and the sterile nuclear medicine unit where I would stop to gather strength for the treatment sessions.

The first few times I stopped I prayed there, embarrassed at my groveling for a longer life. After that I treated it as an oasis—a place to rest and meditate without trying to make a deal with God. But sometime in my wanderings through the tunnel, resting in the oasis and lying like a slab of meat on a slab of something cold and hard, getting zapped by a monster no healthy person wanted to be around, I stumbled onto the process of what is now widely practiced as visualizing. As I lay on the slab listening to the machine howling as it pushed millions of little bits of radiation through my body, I began to envision those bits of radiation zapping whatever cancer cells still dwelled in my body. As the days and weeks of treatment rolled by, my visualizing became more specific. It became a way to justify the side-effects of the radiation—the nausea, diarrhea and fatigue. It became my source of hope that the treatment would cure me.

By early March I was allowed to leave the hospital overnight and I experienced a new fear—the fear of being without the hospital staff on whom I had become dependent for life itself. It was an odd fear, something I didn't anticipate and had not been warned about. Dorene must have thought I was loosing it, when, unable to sleep in my state of panic on that first night away from the hospital, I said I wanted to go back .... now! But I didn't. I fought my way through that night and soon I was able to stay away without panic, but not without fear. Like my close encounters with drowning, it was a long, long time before that nagging fear receded into my subconscious—where recent hospitalizations have revealed it still lurks.

Finally, in June 1963, the medical staff of USNH Bethesda determined they had done all they could for the time being, and discharged me. And the Marine Corps determined that I was too sick to be of any value, so it sent me home with a total disability retirement. My career was over after just three years.

At the age of twenty-four I found myself adrift ... and not exactly in a sea of tranquility. My career plans were ended; I had no job, and probably couldn't get one until I had regained some of my strength. I didn't know how much longer I was going to live, and I had a wife and an almost two-year-old daughter. What to do? I did what any optimist would have done; we moved back to Seattle, bought a house and I started graduate school at the University of Washington.

Friends from my undergraduate days rallied to our support. Walt Ellis, a dear friend for nearly fifty years now, suggested I enroll in a new Masters in Public Administration (MPA) program in which he was enrolling. Our wives were high school buddies; Dorene had been at Rosemary and Walt's wedding, and they had a son our daughter's age. The months of fear and isolation we had lived with in Bethesda, despite the love of the Strengs, was quickly lifting.

With my undergraduate degree in Political Science, the MPA seemed to offer potential as a new career move. These were the days of Project Camelot (see Chapter 10 for more information about this project), and governmental service was seen in a very different light to how it is today. If I couldn't serve my country as a warrior, perhaps I could serve it in some other role. So I began, optimistically, down a new path.

But the fragility of that optimism was soon revealed when I became ill shortly after classes started in September 1963. I had been told when I left Bethesda that if the disease reasserted itself it would either be in my lungs or my brain. The symptoms I suddenly started to experience pointed towards a brain tumor. My world, and my veneer of self-confidence, came crashing down. I lay in a hospital bed at the University of Washington medical school and cried, certain that I was going to die shortly. In the meantime, the medical staff ran all sorts of tests; they came back negative. It was suspected that I had had an attack of a form of encephalitis, but the symptoms disappeared as quickly as they had appeared. I cried again, this time tears of joy. But I had learned another lesson—not to let my optimism cause me to drop my guard. I was in a state of suspended animation and would be for about five years. I could not will the future; I could only operate within some limits of opportunity and hope for the best.

The episode of encephalitis revealed something else: how poorly prepared Dorene and I were for the road ahead. In hindsight, the lack of guidance about how the disease and the treatment had changed our lives was responsible for this. There was not a single consultation with medical staff or social service workers about what to expect and how to deal with changes. Nor had there been any disclosure of the risks the surgery or the radiation treatment presented before treatment began. Jerome Groopman, in his book

The Anatomy of Hope, discusses at length the poor preparation doctors receive in how to communicate with patients and their families who are battling cancer, and how difficult, but important, such communication can be. He believes, as do many physicians these days, that the best decisions are those that are taken jointly by the medical team, patient and family. No one told me there was a ninety per cent chance that I could be impotent following surgery; no one told me that my chances of survival were slim. I found out both of these things much later, and in an off-hand manner. In fact, I learned about survival rates only after I was declared cured, seven years after my treatment at Bethesda. I had come back to Bethesda for a final review, and when that was concluded I was talking with the radiology chief in his office. When the discussion got around to survival rates for my kind of mixed cancer, he opened a file cabinet drawer. In the front were dozens of cases of those who hadn't survived. In the back of the drawer were a handful of survivors. He added my file to this very small group.

No one warned me that the radiation treatment would cause a lifetime of digestive problems, or that the surgery would have permanent side-effects, including the debilitating condition of postural hypotension. When I stand up after sitting or crouching, the normally automatic contraction of blood vessels in my legs does not occur, because the nerves that trigger this response were cut in surgery. The net result is that if I stand up too fast, especially when I'm tired or feeling under the weather, I will black out, but not necessarily lose consciousness. It's a very painful feeling, except on the few occasions I have actually lost consciousness. That of course, can be very dangerous, as I could fall and cause serious damage to myself. But no one warned me about these things; I had to learn them the hard way. No one warned me about the strange attacks I would suffer for several years. I would suddenly start sweating profusely, and my mind would become very confused. I don't know whether they were some form of a panic attack, or something else caused by a hormone imbalance. In any case, even when I reported these attacks during my check-ups at USN Hospitals, nothing was ever explained or done to mitigate them.

For the first few years following my retirement I had to have a medical check-up every six months. That was later extended to an annual check-up. These were not pleasant routines. The procedure I dreaded most was the inferior venacavogram (IVC). In this procedure, a radioactive dye is injected into the femoral vein and then X-rays are taken of the progress of the dye through the kidneys and urinary tract. The dreadful part of the procedure is finding the femoral vein. The physician looks for the vein using a large needle in the groin area. Unfortunately, one of the side-effects of radiation is that it turns normal flesh into leather. To get to a femoral vein, one has to go through several inches of this leather—an extremely painful process. And, in the worst-case scenario, the physician hits the femoral artery instead of the vein. That stops the search for several weeks, until you have healed; then the search starts all over again. After several years of this brutal assault I convinced the medical staff conducting my periodic check-ups that there must be another way to get the same results. They agreed, and the IVC procedure stopped.

1968 was a momentous year for me and for America. For the first time in recent history a sitting president, Lyndon Johnson, was being challenged by members of his own party as a candidate for the presidency. The war in Vietnam was ripping America apart, and the Civil Rights Movement was becoming a part of the anti-war movement, despite important strides made under President Johnson. Then, suddenly, civil unrest exploded into violence, and two of the most powerful voices in America, the Rev. Martin Luther King, Junior, and Bobby Kennedy, were gunned down within months of each other and America's ghettos erupted in violence.

In the midst of this, our family grew with the adoption of our son, Douglas Martin, named for Frederick Douglass and Martin Luther King, Junior. The joy he brought to our family was a welcome relief from the daily barrage of bad news. His arrival was a spur to me to get on with my doctoral studies, which I did by passing my orals and written exams.

But then, Uncle Sam came calling again. In 1968, five years after my diagnosis and treatment, the Marine Corps had a change of heart and decided that I might be of use to them again as a pilot. I suspect that the change of heart had a one-word explanation—Vietnam. Helicopter pilots were now at a premium, given the pressures of the war. My old unit at New River had been one of the first units to go to Vietnam, even before the Gulf of Tonkin Resolution was passed in August of 1964. By 1968 the American commitment to the war in Vietnam was in high gear, and helicopters were a main component of American operations. As they were frequently shot out of the sky, the demand for pilots was great. However, I appealed the intention of the Corps, on obvious medical grounds, and a medical review board wrote the final word on my case—permanent disability retirement. The periodic physical examinations I had undergone through the five-year period also led to the conclusion that I was cured of the cancer. I could pass Go, collect a small retirement check—and get on with my life.

Chapter 10
An Intellectual Awakening

My eyes and my mind had been opened
by our experience of living in Chile
and being forced, in a way,
to look at America from the same perspective
as the rest of the world;
and it wasn't a pretty sight.

Sage Chapel, Cornell University, July 1968.
Doug's interdenominational "dedication" service with Father Daniel Berrigan officiating.

When life starts throwing a change-up pitch to you, you had better be able to make the necessary adjustment, or you're out of the game.

That was the situation in which I found myself in 1963. Plans for a career in the Marine Corps were cut out, literally and figuratively, and so a sudden adjustment was needed. Grad school was a good place to hang out while I re-thought the direction of my life. Having tried my luck at selling encyclopedias as a freshman in college, I knew a career in sales was not a direction I wanted to take. Nor were any of the other part-time jobs I had held in college. Going back to the farm was also out as an option; I already had enough risk in my life. Besides, we were comfortable as a family in the Pacific Northwest. As much as I credited my upbringing among the Pennsylvania Dutch for giving me a great foundation for facing life, I didn't want to go back there; too many bad memories.

The big issue I was facing in 1963 was the realization that I would have to rely on my intellect for making my way in life, rather than other skills. Pondering this brought me to the realization that it was brainpower that had enabled me to get to where I was anyway. I had come to take it for granted, mainly because nothing had been a major intellectual challenge for me up to that point. Sure, I almost flunked out of college during my freshman year, but that was because I hadn't applied myself and not because I couldn't hack the academics. My report cards through primary and secondary education were almost straight As, and by the time I graduated with a BA I had pulled my GPA up to a respectable B+ average.

The MPA program I had enrolled in was broadly interdisciplinary, with coursework in economics, law, political science and sociology. This intellectual stretch forced me to focus on studies, and allowed the issues of my health to recede into the background, but never out of mind. I began to enjoy the fact that intellect was trumping other skills and interests. Since the program was new, there were only four full-time students. And, there were four full-time academic staff members, all veterans of public service as well as being noted academics. This made our seminars demanding and lively. The program had a dozen or more part-time students who were already in public service careers, which added flavor to class interaction, and I found this environment challenging and rewarding.

During the first year of grad school I also had the opportunity to work as a graduate teaching assistant for one of the professors in the political science department. My primary role was to grade tests and term papers, and hold study groups where students could raise questions about matters they didn't understand. This gave me insights into the aspects of academic life that deals with how students and professors communicate, and I found myself emulating Mrs Bossard of Gravers School more than Professor Warren, and with good results.

The full-time MPA students were required to serve a year-long internship during the second year of our program, as well as carrying a regular academic load. My internship was with the University of Washington's Bureau of Governmental Research and Service, and I was engaged in a research project documenting the scope of services offered by all the municipalities in the State of Washington—an activity that led to my first academic publication. However, the most exciting event that happened during my tenure at the Bureau was the day Seattle experienced a significant earthquake. My office was above the boiler room, and I thought the boiler had exploded. I ran to the back door of the Bureau, in time to watch parked cars doing a dance in the parking lot, and utility poles and wires swinging in rhythm to the dancing cars. It was my first earthquake ... and I was impressed! It sure beat the fierce thunder and lightning storms nature threw our way on the farm ... even the storm in 1947 when lightning struck our house, our barn and a power transformer all on the same night.

As both the end of the spring term of 1965 and graduation approached, I was selected to be in Cornell University's Latin American Internship Program, a new venture funded by the Ford Foundation as a way to promote interest among new graduates of professional schools with career opportunities in Latin America. A crash course at Cornell in Spanish language and Latin American culture, politics and economics during the summer of 1965 gave the twelve interns and their spouses a foundation on which to undertake one to two years of living and working in Latin America.

I had selected Chile as our home for the immediate future, primarily because it was the only South American country I had the slightest knowledge of, based on the short visit I had made there as a midshipman years earlier.

So, in August of 1965 our little family boarded a flight from JFK to Buenos Aires, where we spent the night, mostly recovering from the scariest taxi ride I had ever had in my life. The next day we flew over the Andes and landed in Santiago. It was the middle of winter, and in the shadow of the Andes, Santiago can be cold, but our room in the lovely Hotel Carerra was comfortable and inviting. The hotel was the focal point of Chile's social and political life, as it had the pride of place on Santiago's main square, next to the Presidential Palace. Chile had just elected Eduardo Frei as President, the first left-of-center party to hold that office in the country's history, and many viewed the new administration with the same hopes that Jack Kennedy had brought to Washington four years earlier.

During our stay at the Carerra the president of Italy made a state visit and from our window on the square, we watched the pageantry as the horse-drawn carriages carrying the two presidents made their way right beneath us. An honor guard in uniforms reminiscent of 19th century troops marched briskly by while a military band played stirring martial music.

The dining-room of the Carerra had its share of important visitors, many on missions from international donor agencies anxious to work closely with the Christian Democratic administration of President Frei. One particular individual, an American woman, was taken by our flaxen haired four-year-old daughter, who could only sit quietly for a limited time. Soon, we began sharing a table with Dorothy Major, the American woman. She was in Chile on a mission for the World Health Organization. Those wonderful times in the Carerra developed into a life-long friendship with Dorothy, who was a force to be reckoned with in nursing education in the United States.

We settled briefly into a neat little house on Calle Jorge Matte, in a middle-class suburb, but the day-long commotion among the turkeys in the neighbor's backyard drove us away to another, larger house in Santiago's Barrio Alto. There was a primary school a block away and a neighborhood of children, and soon our daughter was in first grade at the tender age of four and a half—the only "gringa" in the whole school. At first she seemed to be struggling with Spanish, until we learned that she thought that if she spoke Spanish she wouldn't be able to speak to us in English any more! As soon as we assured her that she could speak both, her fluency quickly surpassed that of her parents' combined.

My internship was in the University of Chile's faculty of economics, in the Institute of Organization and Administration (INSORA). I was assigned to a team working on a model to determine the state of readiness among Chile's municipalities for increased autonomy from the central government. The Christian Democrats had campaigned on a broad platform of increased participation by Chile's citizens in governmental affairs, and municipal autonomy was one dimension of this thrust. Other dimensions included increased rights of workers, education reform and, most ambitious of all, a plan to break up some of Chile's large, unproductive farms and to give land ownership to the peasants, many of whom still lived and worked in feudal conditions.

My primary counterpart in this research project was a Chilean, Jorge Lopez, who had just returned to Chile after completing an MPA at Cornell. Our families became friends and during our first summer in Chile they invited us to spend a few days in the village of Rio Claro where Sonia, Jorge's wife, had grown up. The village was near the southern end of Chile's beautiful Central Valley. This region was devastated on May 22, 1960 by the strongest earthquake ever recorded, measuring 9.5 on the Richter scale. But despite its power, relatively few people were killed because it had been preceded by a number of smaller quakes, and people in towns and villages, like Rio Claro, spent most of their days and nights outside, in open spaces.

Mama Rosa, Sonia's mother, described what those days were like: as the earthquakes grew in number and intensity, a kind of mass hysteria took hold of the people every time the earth began shaking. Once a tremor had stopped, a level of calm returned, but never at the same level as before the last earthquake. This process of ratcheting up hysteria continued for over a week, and then the big one hit. At that point many people "lost it". It was many months before life returned to normal. When we drove through the region, five years after the Big One, the physical damage was still starkly visible. And, I imagine that if a quake had occurred while we were there, we would have seen old psychological fault lines immediately revealed.

Chile is an exceptionally beautiful country, and we explored as much of it as we could on our limited budget. Dorene's mother spent several months with us, and during that time we rented a camper and drove to the southern end of the Pan American highway, to the town of Puerto Montt. This incredibly beautiful town, even with its visible scars from the 1960 earthquake, is on an inlet of the Pacific Ocean and its port is the lifeline that connects all the towns further south with the rest of Chile. We spent hours at the waterfront watching the fascinating process of transferring materials from the docks to donkey carts. The donkeys then pulled their carts out to the ships, where they were unloaded, and the donkeys returned for another load. This was the way things had been done in the old days before the docks and modern equipment replaced the donkeys, but when the earthquake destroyed much of the harbor facilities, the old way became the new way again, and the donkeys and their drivers moved back to center stage.

Our trip took us through the countryside of south-central Chile, where active volcanoes dominate the landscape, and where the Mapuche Indians, Chile's indigenous people, were forced to live following their violent suppression by Spanish colonists in the 19th century. When we visited the area, the Chilean Government, which had forced the Mapuches onto reservations like the US Government, was trying to improve their living conditions by building new houses for them. The Mapuches responded by using the houses as barns for their animals. We met some of the Maryknoll missionaries who were working with the Mapuches, who told us about unjust treatment the indigenous people of the Americas have suffered at the hands of the colonizers. The Maryknolls, a Catholic Order that was founded in the 20th century, is devoted exclusively to working with indigenous peoples on the continent. Later, as I reflected on that casual meeting with this unique order, I realized that it awakened my awareness of the great divide between the have and have-nots of the world, and the insidious role my country had sometimes played in creating and sustaining this divide.

This realization was part of the intellectual awakening that had begun in graduate school, but in Chile it was being driven by the unique awareness of one's self and one's cultural blindness when living abroad and learning to see one's countrymen as others see us. In the sixties it was easy to assume much of the world loved us Americans. That assumption was reinforced whenever we were invited into the homes of Chileans, especially in working-class homes. Often, there would be two pictures—one of either Jesus or the Pope, and one of Jack Kennedy.

Apparently, pictures of Jack Kennedy and the Pope adorned many homes in Ireland, but that was to be expected, given Kennedy's Irish Catholic background—but in the homes of lower-class Chileans was entirely unexpected, at least by me. It speaks of the great reservoir of affection many people worldwide had for America in the early 1960s. Some of that affection was carried over from our role in World War II, and the economic assistance our government gave to post-war reconstruction efforts in Europe. Some of it was tied to the continuing belief that America was the land of opportunity, open to all who went there and were willing to work hard. And as I think back to those pictures of Jack Kennedy on the walls of people in Latin America, Europe, Africa and Asia, I cannot help but wonder how many homes in those far corners of the world have pictures of George Bush. I expect there to be far fewer, and this is a direct reflection on how perceptions of America and our leaders have changed.

As my own perception became more acute in Chile in 1965, and as my language skills improved, I began to recognize an undercurrent of discontent regarding America. It was directed primarily towards the American private sector, which was seen to be exploiting the people of Latin America. In Chile, this meant primarily the copper industry, which was dominated by American interests. But other examples were pointed out—oil in Venezuela, fruit in Central America, the auto industry throughout the continent, the travel industry, et cetera. And in Chile, America was shouldering its way into the food industry in the form of a Rockefeller-owned supermarket chain that was rapidly expanding, as it had in Argentina, at the expense of the little neighborhood specialty shops—the butcher, the baker, the wine shop, the green grocer—which were all threatened by the American supermarkets springing up near the middle- and upper-class residential areas.

For the moment, there was ambivalence about American foreign policy because the Kennedy administration had launched, with great fanfare, the "Alliance for Progress", which was seen by many as the first genuine effort of the US government to try to address some of the economic woes of Latin America. However, by 1967, when we left Chile, many Chileans regarded the Alliance differently, and cleverly used the Spanish language to show this. In Spanish the Alliance for Progress is "La Allianza para Progresso". However, the word "para", besides being the preposition "for", is also the third person singular of the verb "to stop". So, by 1967 when Chileans said, "la Allianza para progresso", they were increasingly implying that the Alliance *stops* progress, and they would share their experiences of American foreign-aid bureaucracy which belied the proclaimed intent of the program.

As I rode public transportation to work each day, I became much more aware of the subtle racial or ethnic discrimination that exists, even today, in Latin America. The US can't be held responsible for this—it was Latin America's own human shortcoming. The darker the skin one has, the more likely one experiences all kinds of discrimination. Some of the bus routes I rode on started on the fringes of the urban areas, where the poorest of the poor—and the darkest skinned—lived. As the route approached the center of town, the passengers became fair-skinned. Chile has a large northern European population, as many families of Germans and English descent immigrated there during the 19th and early 20th centuries. Chile's first president following their independence from Spain was a man by the name of O'Higgins. Most of my colleagues at INSORA were fair-skinned. The head of the Department of Public Administration was a northern Italian who was practically blond. A leading economist in the faculty was very dark-skinned and he was called "El Negrito". Despite his intellectual productivity he would never become Dean, as he was said to be "too dark".

Meanwhile in America, the mid-sixties saw our own troubled efforts to deal with racism—efforts that were complicated by the deepening involvement in Vietnam. Despite the ostensible equity suggested by the draft, the reality was that if you were poor or black, the draft was going to get you, but if you were white and had access to sufficient wealth to go to college, you could get a deferment.

When we returned home to the USA in September 1967, we saw a very different America to the country we had left in 1965. Granted, there had been major changes—the war, the civil rights movement and the many false starts of the "great society"—but perhaps the biggest change was that my perspective—the cognitive perch from which I looked at America—had fundamentally shifted. My eyes and my mind had been opened by our experience of living in Chile and being forced, in a way, to look at America from the same perspective as the rest of the world; and it wasn't a pretty sight.

We returned, not to the culturally comfortable confines of suburban Seattle, but to the emotionally charged atmosphere of Cornell University. I entered a Ph.D. program there in Public Administration, with minors in Latin American Studies and Development Administration. Cornell had a strong program in Latin American studies, with a decidedly leftist orientation. What I had experienced in Latin America could now be better understood, analytically, from a theoretical perspective. I now understood the Maryknolls within the context of liberation theology. And the opposition to the Vietnam War on the Cornell campus had a strong focus shaped by the quiet but poetically powerful voice of Father Daniel Berrigan, S.J., and a faculty member in Cornell's Campus Ministry program.

Daniel Berrigan, a Jesuit priest who had established himself as a poet of unusual talent, and his brother Philip, a priest in the Josephite Order, became iconic anti-war/peace activist figures in the late sixties. They led a number of anti-war demonstrations, highlighted by the destruction of some Selective Service files in Catonsville, Maryland, by pouring their own blood over the files. For this they were tried and sentenced to prison. Both wrote extensively about their beliefs and their experiences, and I was hardly alone in being influenced by their position and their passion.

Daniel Berrigan's passionate poetry lit a fire in me that forged a bond between intellect and emotion greater than anything I had ever experienced before in my life. And the amazing thing was that Daniel was such a quiet, peaceful person, yet when one listened carefully to what he was saying, one could not help being struck by the emotional force of his words, whether or not one agreed with him. One night, after having spent several hours with a group of students discussing the Vietnam War with Daniel and listening to him read and discuss some of his poetry about personal responsibility to speak out against injustices, I went home and had a powerful dream about writing poetry. It was as close to a "calling" as I had ever felt, and the next day I wrote my first real poem (as opposed to the "Roses are red, Violets are blue" variety):

Daniel Berrigan, S.J.
I dream of Abstraction
who was a man
with features both sharp and blurred
as were his actions
and his meaning.

At times his eyes spoke
To me and to all with a tenderness
That turned the heads
Of the deaf and dumb.

At times his eyes could not be seen
And men of reason passed him by
Ignoring his existence and his calling.

I tossed, disturbed
By the pains of conscience
As Abstraction told in language simple
And honest action
Of the tragedy of man.

I tossed, disturbed
By the pains of ignorance
As Abstraction spoke with soundless words
and actions that did not move.

And then the dawn came
And with it
The eternal darkness.

Richard Fehnel—October 10, 1968

In the months that followed I wrote more poetry, and as Daniel's actions led him to civil disobedience I contemplated following his lead. However, I felt constrained by the obligation to support my family, which had now grown to four with the adoption of our son Douglas Martin in April 1968.

That summer Daniel led an ecumenical christening ceremony for our son in the chapel at Cornell. It was a simple but moving ceremony, with contributions from friends from different religions, and an appropriate homily from Father Daniel. After the ceremony we went to his modest apartment for lunch. The atmosphere at lunch was somewhat tense initially because Dorothy Major, our friend from Chile who now lived in Albany New York, was a Catholic who saw Berrigan and his brother Joseph as unpatriotic heretics. So did another couple that had participated in the christening. But Daniel, in his quiet, perceptive way, put all at ease. The christening, as I recall, was just after Daniel's famous trip to Hanoi, during which he negotiated the release of three American POWs.

I finished my coursework, passed my orals and comprehensive exams, and began designing the research that would form the basis of my dissertation. I wanted to examine the role of universities in Chile and Brazil in furthering the development objectives which the governments in those two countries were pursuing. My research would be based on in-depth interviews with students, faculty members, and the administrators and governmental planners who were designing development plans. It was an overly ambitious research project, both intellectually and operationally. I was fortunate to receive a Fulbright grant, which covered most of my costs of traveling to Chile and Brazil, as well as the costs of the research activities.

I went to Chile first, and started the process of translating questionnaires into Spanish and making arrangements for the fieldwork. What I hadn't taken into account, however, was Chile's slide from the heady early days of the Frei Administration to the days of political infighting between the Christian Democrats, who controlled the lower house of Congress, and the coalition of other political parties including the Socialists and Communists on the left, and the parties on the right. The coalition controlled the Senate and effectively blocked the legislative agenda of the Frei administration.

The municipal autonomy legislation that I had worked on several years earlier was dead, as were many other progressive reforms. As a consequence, there was political turmoil in the country. University students went on strike in protest against the government's inaction. In return, the universities were closed for weeks on end, and my study was jeopardized. Compounding the situation was an understandable air of paranoia among many in the university community concerning an American study of the role of universities in development. Their concerns were fueled by the revelations of Project Camelot, a US Department of Defense study seeking to "determine the feasibility of developing a general social systems model which would make it possible to predict and influence politically significant aspects of social change in the developing nations of the world". Latin America in general, and Chile in particular, was targeted by this study, and it created an understandable furor.

Fortunately, I had established my credibility sufficiently through my previous work at the University of Chile, so with the assistance of creative researchers, we were finally able to conduct enough interviews to have a statistically significant sampling of students, faculty and administrators and government planners. However, I had blown my research budget in the meantime and was unable to include Brazilian universities in my research.

I completed my research, left Chile and returned to Ithaca a few months before the Chilean presidential elections of 1970 that saw Salvador Allende, the head of the Chilean Socialist Party, elected as President. Three years later, on September 11, 1973, President Allende died during the military take-over of the government, and Chile's long history of democracy—the longest in South America it was claimed—came to a bloody and violent end.

My five-year involvement with Chile had a profound effect upon me. It had given me the opportunity to see a world vastly different in many respects to the world I knew. It had forced me to think about issues and causes I hadn't considered much before, especially the pervasiveness of so much injustice directed towards the poor, the marginalized, the voiceless people of the Americas, including North America. It had awakened in me passions I had not felt before and, through Daniel Berrigan, a vehicle for expressing some of that passion. At their core, the values I had acquired on the farm and in

Gravers School had not only been validated, I now found how aptly they applied to a larger canvas of life than I had previously realized, and that realization guided me towards a form of academic activism that I was to follow for the rest of my professional life.

Chapter 11
Academe

I TAUGHT THEM THEORY AND THEY TAUGHT ME
REALITY—A CLASSIC WIN-WIN SITUATION ...
THE POWER OF LEARNING BY DOING,
WHICH MRS BOSSARD HAD TAUGHT ME IN GRAVERS
SCHOOL, HAD EVEN MORE POWER IN THE
"PURE" AIR OF ACADEME.

Late 1960s / early 1970s.
Assisstant Professor at American University, Washington, DC.

The American University Years (1969–1973)

Even with a wet handkerchief covering my nose and mouth, the tear-gas burned in my throat. My eyes watered and burned as well, but I went up the stairs of the Ward Circle Building to my office. Protesting students were using the building's lobby as a command center, because this building on the American University (AU) campus was adjacent to an important traffic circle in northwest Washington, DC. The students were protesting against the latest tactical operation of the Nixon administration in the Vietnam War. The students were aiming to disrupt rush hour traffic on this important artery, where Massachusetts Avenue crossed Nebraska Avenue. They knew the Washington, DC police would not follow them onto the campus, but they hadn't reckoned with the use of tear-gas to drive them off the circle.

I had participated in numerous protest marches in downtown DC since we moved to Bethesda in the fall of 1969. But as the war dragged on and the casualties mounted, the protests nationwide grew more violent. Even the sleepy, conservative American University, not known as a hotbed of passions of any kind, and certainly not of politics, was now in the thick of things and grabbing regional headlines because of its students.

As I picked my way around the students who were scattered around the lobby floor and up the stairways, I thought about the irony of the situation. Just recently I had switched from being a full-time program officer in the Institute of Public Administration (IPA—the nation's oldest public policy think-tank) and part-time academic at the American University to being a full-time academic at AU and a part-time program officer for IPA. The irony was that in my program officer role my office was on Connecticut Avenue, between DuPont Circle and the White House, a route frequently used by the many protest marches. Many businesses on Connecticut Avenue, including two in our building, had decided it was easier to leave the plywood sheets in place on their display windows rather than putting them up and taking them down practically every weekend.

And I thought that by moving to the AU campus I would find a little more tranquility, and be able to make more progress on my dissertation!

On this particular late afternoon, apparently forewarned by the DC police, the President of the AU had rapidly distributed a letter (in the days before e-mail) to all faculty members saying that they had the option of cancelling classes that evening or using the class time to discuss the war and the protests. My class was a graduate seminar in comparative bureaucracy, and the students ranged from a few typical grad students who had just finished their undergraduate degrees and were pursuing graduate studies (probably to avoid the draft), to a number of students who were mid-career bureaucrats, working on an MPA or a doctorate. Several of the mid-careerists were military officers working at the Pentagon, and generally came to class in uniform because our classes started at 5 or 6 p.m. and they didn't have time to change. I had begun to wonder whether some of them were also avoiding deployment to Vietnam by matriculating in an advanced degree program, knowing that they were unlikely to be transferred away from DC before they finished the degree (which Uncle Sam was paying for).

At the start of the semester I had introduced the class to the use of a "visual I Ching" as a device to focus and "ration" discussion. It was a teaching tool developed by the Yale School of Architecture, as I recall, and one of my colleagues at the IPA, an architect, introduced it to me. I began using it when it seemed the class was drifting.

The visual I Ching is a large collage—I used a cardboard box a mattress had come in—made up of photos taken mainly from magazine ads, selected for their ability to provoke ideas and feelings. The discussants (a class, a public meeting, a committee, etc.) need to come to an agreement on one question that deals with the issue at hand. Then each discussant is given a half dozen stickpins; and each person has differently colored pins. With the guiding question in mind, the discussants mill around the collage and stick pins into photos that suggest an answer to or an aspect of the chosen question. When they have finished, each discussant removes the pins one at a time and briefly explains what the photo elicited in the way of a response to the question. No questions or discussion by other discussants is allowed, except to clarify a point. As each person relates his or her points, a person records the essence of each point on a blackboard or flip chart. The process continues until they have all had their say. At that point, they focus on the recorded comments. The comments that agree with each other are noted first. Then they focus on the comments that indicate areas of disagreement and frame a guiding question that addresses the most important area of disagreement among the discussants, and the I Ching is "interrogated" again. Generally, by the third or fourth go, they will have eliminated major areas of disagreement, and have a record of the areas of agreement.

I had used the I Ching several times with this class, so they were comfortable with it. There were obvious areas of disagreement among the students around the Vietnam conflict, which was an underlying source of tension among them. The Pentagon students clearly had one point of view; the younger, straight-out-of-undergraduate-school students had another.

On this particular night, when we were all settled in, with windows wide open to defuse the remaining traces of tear gas, I read the letter from the AU president and asked the class what they wanted to do. The initial reaction was to cancel the class, but then someone suggested using the I Ching. I sent two of the students to my office to get it, while we began trying to identify a guiding question that wasn't "loaded" towards one group or the other. As suggestions were made I wrote them on the blackboard, and after about fifteen minutes of discussions, clarifications and amendments we came up with a guiding question that all had agreed to. Today, around thirty-five years after this particular class session, I can't remember what the question was but the students eagerly began sticking their pins in the board, and the process began. Some two hours later, after several rounds of questions, the class broke up—in relative harmony. The mental snapshot I will carry forever is the conversation between a colonel and the most radical student in the class—a bearded type—acknowledging that for the first time they understood each other as they headed off to have a beer together and continue their conversation.

I've gone on quite a bit about this particular class session because it was an epiphany for me, and for the students. It demonstrated that regardless of the context—and the emotions were running high at the start of the class that night—people holding widely differing views could be brought to a point where they are able to "hear" each other, and are able to use that hearing to build bridges of communication. Furthermore, it showed me that I had a critical role to play as a facilitator of learning without having to know all the answers.

During the course, it became clear that while I knew the theories behind different approaches for analyzing bureaucracies in a comparative way, many of the students had much deeper knowledge regarding how various bureaucracies actually worked. So I made a deal with them; I taught them theory and they taught me reality—a classic win-win situation. In my academic career I kept running into professors who treated the world as if they knew about it or were expected to. As a result, they were too scared to admit to students that they—the students—might know more about some of the subject matter than the professors. The students' knowledge was based on experience, and their experiences had shown them which theories worked and which didn't and under what circumstances. The power of learning by doing, which Mrs Bossard had taught me in Gravers School, had even more power in the "pure" air of academe.

I was enjoying teaching; most of the graduate students at the American University were working adults with full-time jobs. They knew how to focus and how to use their limited studying time efficiently. Assignments were submitted when due, and at a standard that was comparable to the graduate level at Cornell University. Teaching undergraduates, however, was a different story. Many were from upper middle-class, urban, families from the East who had failed to get into their first choice college. So they came to class with "an attitude" that didn't fit my approach to teaching, which required a high level of initiative and activity on the part of students. On the other hand, most of my colleagues in the school of government and public administration and in the school of international studies were stimulating and generally open to my enthusiasm for trying new things in the classroom. We experimented with team teaching and with new courses. I began work on a book with a colleague in the school of international studies and a colleague in the economics department.

Despite the ongoing trauma of the war, and the almost weekly routine of protest marches in Washington, DC, we were enjoying our move to Bethesda. The local farmers' market, an institution that I believe is still going strong, almost made up for the move from rural Ithaca. I missed our frequent visits to the agricultural school at Cornell, where our children could see piglets and newly born calves and sheep. They thought I was crazy when I said that the smell of manure made me happy. I also missed the view from the kitchen window of our little house on Richard Place in Ithaca which looked out across the town of Ithaca towards that special place high above Cayuga's waters, where the farmlands of Tompkins County snuggled comfortably against the great lawns and oak trees of the university, just as Ezra Cornell had envisioned. In the winter the view in the early morning was special—smoke rising lazily from dozens of chimneys in the town below, letting me know I wasn't the first to rise, while snow-covered fields, as far as the eye could see, kept their blankets of white pulled snugly against the fences and hedges that bordered the fields.

But Bethesda had offered new opportunities not only to me, but to the rest of the family as well. Our Sunday morning routine became a trip to the Smithsonian, staying only as long as the children were enjoying this renowned educational facility. Summer evenings included a walk to Gifford's ice-cream parlor on Wisconsin Avenue, another local institution. Perhaps because of the transient nature of life in Washington, DC, it seemed much easier for us to make friends than in Ithaca, where only one neighborhood family had gone out of their way to welcome us. Even the FBI agent and his family, who lived next door, were welcoming, despite the posters of Daniel Berrigan—now an underground fugitive following his conviction in Catonsville— that we had put up in our family-room.

But as the seasons passed we began to realize that living in Bethesda on an assistant professor's modest salary had serious limitations. We would not be able to buy a house unless I was willing to commute several hours a day ... and I wasn't interested in that peculiar form of American torture. Besides, we were becoming increasingly concerned about the growing drug culture in the suburbs of DC. A colleague and I had carried out a grant from the Sloan Foundation to study heroin use in the metropolitan area—one of a number of cities covered by the study. Our findings contradicted the basic assumptions of the study—that heroin addiction was primarily a problem of black males. We found that in the Washington, DC area it was a rapidly growing problem of white adolescents, and high schools were the venue of "action". We even found cases of use by AU students. Alarmingly, no one seemed to recognize the problem. The media focused on heroin use in the black ghetto of DC and ignored what was happening in the suburbs. Furthermore, I was becoming annoyed by the structure of the curriculum, which provided little opportunity for internships. Here we were in the middle of Washington, yet our public affairs curriculum could have been designed for an institution that was in the middle of the boonies. Internships arranged by our school were mainly in the summer, when Washington falls asleep, and carried no academic credit. My proposals to put students in government agencies, non-profit organizations, lobbying organizations and the growing number of DC-based think-tanks fell on deaf ears in the curriculum committee.

Nor was I making much progress on my dissertation. Holding two jobs, one of which involved several new course preparations a year, kept me away from my own studies for long periods, precisely at a time when it demanded sustained attention. And I was growing increasingly uneasy with the realization that the rest of the country didn't matter much to the policy-makers in Washington, DC, despite Nixon's commitment to stronger rights for states. The war in Vietnam understandably distorted how everything was perceived, but Washington's tone deafness seemed to be spreading to other issues besides the war. My sensitivity, as a result of my Latin American experience, towards how US foreign policy was being perverted by undemocratic ideals now seemed to be tuning in to similar misgivings about domestic policy. I felt a need to find a home, in intellectual and family terms, where we could live closer to what constituted my somewhat romantic notion of American ideals. So we began to look "homeward"—to the Northwest, for job opportunities.

The University of Oregon Years (1973–1978)

Our search ended with an attractive offer from the University of Oregon. A new professional school in community service and public affairs had been started with a commitment to teaching and research that was grounded in the needs of the community. The heart of the school's curriculum was the attempted linkage between theory and practice, between coursework and internships. And the soul of the school was its commitment to older learners, those seeking a second chance to finish a college degree. To me, the approach of the school was an answer to my unease with traditional approaches to learning in higher education, and to the need to give greater access to those who really were motivated to learn.

To our family, Eugene, Oregon offered a new approach to living: miles of bike paths and hiking trails in town; a city park next door to our house; my office a ten minute walk from home (a lovely architect-designed house that we could actually afford to buy); schools for the children within easy and safe walking distance; and a community spirit that was both laid back and aggressively committed to citizen involvement. Eugene in the early 1970s was the "track capital" of the USA, and Steve Prefontaine, the world's best distance runner at the time, was its poster child. Eugene was also probably the hippy capital of the USA, a reputation it bore somewhat ambivalently. The lush mountain valleys around Eugene were home to dozens of communes and those seeking a peacefully independent life style. Ken Kesey, the dairy farmer and writer, who lived in nearby Springfield was at his zenith, and his psychedelic bus was sighted frequently at rural gatherings. Eugene's newly launched "Saturday Market" was where you went for tie-dyed material, macramé plant hangers, scented candles and locally grown produce, including a suspiciously wide range of mushrooms. As the day wore on, the air at the Saturday Market was often thick with the sweet smell of marijuana. That should have warned us about the dangers that lurked in this seemingly idyllic community, dangers that would come to haunt us years later.

My position at the university was exactly what I had been searching for; it offered a rich opportunity for curricular experimentation and research that soon led to numerous grants and publications with similarly minded colleagues. The school of community service and public affairs encouraged consulting work with public sector organizations striving to improve the quality of service offered to citizens, and a colleague and I soon launched a consulting practice that gained a reputation for practical innovations to enhance state and local welfare agencies' ability to deliver services.

The research grants and publications which colleagues and I had produced in experiential learning and higher education programs for "non-traditional learners" gained national attention. But as is often the case, the prophet is not recognized in his homeland. And contrary to the University of Oregon's public image as a liberal university, I soon discovered that the so-called education liberals at this institution were defiantly resistant to educational innovations that attempted curricular reform. The three years that I chaired the university-wide Educational Innovations Committee were among the most frustrating experiences I ever had in committee work in any organizational setting. The efforts colleagues and I had launched to bring about curricular changes in line with changes being adopted by universities leading the country in innovations were stopped short.

The irony of the situation has a somewhat humorous expression in the following story. On graduation day in 1977 or 1978, I was standing in the academic processional, with Norm Sundberg, my principal co-author and the first dean of the school of community service and public affairs with an outstanding academic reputation. The line wasn't moving so we had time to chat. Across the street from where we were standing was Eugene's Pioneer Cemetery. The City and the University were negotiating the removal of this hallowed ground to another location so the University could expand. As we looked at the cemetery and lamented the intransigence of the academics in this supposedly liberal university, we had the same thought—it's easier to move a cemetery than to change a university. This became the theme-setting "quotation" in our next publication—a case study on why academics resist change.

While these transformation efforts were being thwarted on my own campus, I was having success in introducing changes at other institutions in the state. With a grant from Oregon's Educational Co-ordination Commission, I had formed a consortium of thirteen institutions—two-year and four-year, public and private institutions. Through the consortium, we were assisting interested institutions in developing the state's awareness of the need for programs providing working adults with access to higher education. And as that awareness spread, we assisted them in examining different models for non-traditional learners and in initiating pilot programs that fit the particular missions of different institutions.

The process was actually fun. During one period I rented a winnebago and travelled the state with a group of national experts, conducting workshops for faculty staff and administrators at interested institutions. My passion for institutional changes that addressed the needs of working adults had been ignited by Dr Morris Keeton, the president of CAEL, a newly formed consortium of roughly four hundred colleges and universities with a common interest in the educational needs of working adults. Morris was that organization's "glue" due to his passion, dedication and, above all, his quiet determination to bring quality to the work of CAEL. Up until that time, many institutions had provided programs for working adults because they represented a fast market. Morris's efforts were the opposite. He discouraged seeing these programs as cash cows. Instead he assisted the institutions in becoming generators of high quality experiential learning programs that facilitated the educational advancement of working adults. I had the honor, thanks to Morris, of being on the first national board for quality assurance in experiential learning in higher education and I spent many hours with him and other board members developing guidelines that would help realize institutional interests and also serve to reassure the regional accrediting association that CAEL member institutions needed to be acknowledged and reaffirmed.

Not only was Morris a great organizer, he was also renowned for his ability to charm funding organizations out of considerable amounts of money. These funds he used to establish national research programs which would help document the practices that universities and colleges were using with regard to the awarding of credit for prior learning, as well as credit for current sponsored internships. At one point the University of Oregon held three such grants from CAEL, the only university to have achieved that distinction and, as I recall, I was the principal researcher in all three. I suggested earlier that a prophet isn't recognized in his own land, and in my case, this had become true. However, I was being recognized in the State of Oregon and beyond for the innovative approach I was lobbying for.

The Linfield Years (1978–1983)

One of the places that recognized my innovations in program development was Linfield College, a small private traditional liberal arts college that was a member of the consortium of institutions I had founded. Linfield had a visionary as the founding father of a degree program for non-traditional learners. Dr John Day, a physicist by profession, had helped Linfield create a small off-campus program offering a bachelor of arts in liberal studies to registered nurses who were under increasing pressure to have a baccalaureate degree as well as their nursing certificate. John had started this program several years earlier, but was having difficulty in getting the college to support its expansion. Furthermore, because of his age, he was looking for someone to take the program over from him, and he encouraged me to apply for the newly created position of dean of off-campus programs and continuing education at Linfield. I applied, and was selected for the position. I finally had a platform from which I could begin to put into motion those ideas for which I had been lobbying for several years, not only within the University of Oregon but across the state.

Linfield had been pushed in the direction of finding new markets of students because its traditional on-campus liberal arts program, had been encountering financial difficulties. As was the case with many traditional liberal arts colleges around the country, the solution was found in the new market of non-traditional learners. Linfield had just hired a new president, Charles Walker, who was familiar with this latest trend and was anxious to see Linfield develop its fledgling bachelor of arts program in liberal studies into something more robust and not exclusively limited to registered nurses. So when I joined Linfield, I had strong support from the President to push forward with the development of new programs that would produce revenues in excess of the cost as well as deliver a high quality product. I reported directly to the vice-president for academic affairs, John Housley. Over the next three years I learned more from Jack about political management in educational institutions than I had ever known. It was through his careful mentoring, coaching and strategizing that Linfield was able to offer what ultimately turned out to be the most creative degree program for working adults in the State of Oregon. Jack taught me how to identify the opinion-leaders in the relevant departments and get them on my side, so that when issues came to a vote in the entire faculty, the vote had essentially already been won. We expanded the degree program by adding to the bachelor of arts in liberal studies a bachelor of systems management and a bachelor of management. These programs appealed to numbers of people in Oregon's growing hi-tech industry, as well as in general management fields.

By 1983 graduating students from Linfield's off-campus program were the second largest cohort of any graduating class, second only to students in the on-campus business major. The profile of the off-campus graduate from 1980 onward demonstrated that the program goal of addressing a wide range of potential adult learners had been met. Registered nurses were still an important component, but graduates now included bank managers, employees in Oregon's fast growing silicone forest, managerial staff in public utilities, and a few retired people who wanted a degree in order to finish old, unfinished business. Undoubtedly, my favorite student in this latter category was Ruth Hickock, who was nearing ninety years of age when she earned her degree in the off-campus program. She had been a student at Linfield as a teenager back in the days when it was possible to pay your tuition in walnuts. Her husband had served as Linfield president, but she never finished her degree, which had always bothered her. So when the off-campus program was started, with course schedules and venues of instruction that were developed around the needs of working adults, it provided her the opportunity to fulfil her dream. She was living in a retirement home in Salem and was able to either take classes on the weekend or attend some of the classes in our Salem office. On graduation day, in the special festivities that followed the awarding of degrees, I asked her what her plans were now that this goal had been met. She looked at me as if I had just asked her a really stupid question. And her reply confirmed it, "Why, to get my master's degree, of course."

Many of the graduates of the off-campus program did pursue graduate studies, and I felt that the off-campus program should address this need. The Board of Trustees, however, was reluctant to move in this direction. The off-campus program had grown quickly and we needed to consolidate our gains and pursue the details from numerous policy initiatives. Now, more clearly than ever, I became aware of my own strengths and weaknesses. My strength lay in taking ideas and giving them shape, my weakness lay in developing the administrative details essential to good program implementation. I was a better than average grant writer and, in fact, had taught courses in grant writing at the University of Oregon. After writing successful grants or proposals, I was happy to turn over implementation of the grants to others. I was enthusiastic about developing new courses, but after teaching the same course more than two or three times, it became boring. This insight interested me. In growing up on the farm I had learned the importance of getting the job done correctly the first time, so attention to detail was not a foreign concept to me, but as I grew older I found that the "chase" was the source of my enthusiasm. When the chase was over, the enthusiasm quickly waned.

When my boss and mentor, Jack Housley, died in 1983, I applied for his position, vice-president of academic affairs and was disappointed when I didn't get it. It was the first time in my life I didn't get a job that I had applied for. But, in retrospect, it was the right move by the selection committee to select someone else. Jack and President Walker had masterfully initiated many new academic programs at Linfield. These new programs and their features had brought Linfield national recognition. What was needed now in academic affairs was a person with the attention to detail that I had little interest in. The off-campus program had grown considerably and I had also introduced Elderhostel programs at Linfield and, in fact, to the State of Oregon. Their development needed further attention, as did a number of other innovations that the college had undertaken. With Jack, I had negotiated Linfield taking over The Good Samaritan Hospital School of Nursing, and started the curricular process of developing a BSN program at Linfield's new "Portland Campus". But, as I said, in retrospect, I was not the right choice for following through on these matters. So, when former colleagues at the American University contacted me in the summer of 1983 about rejoining them as a consultant on a World Bank funded project in Bangladesh, I was ready to leave academe behind and return to the world of consulting on a full-time basis.

Accepting the position at Linfield had meant moving away from Eugene and various other family changes. As junior faculty member at the University of Oregon, our entertainment expectations were limited and meant mostly socializing with other junior faculty members and students. Steve Greenwood, one of my first students there, who together with his wife, Lynn, have become close family friends, recently reminded me of the frequent student gatherings at our house in Eugene where we watched the Watergate hearings.

The move to Linfield as a dean meant increased and diverse entertaining events. Dorene managed this transition smoothly, even under trying circumstances. We frequently recall, and are now able to laugh at, one such trying evening: the dinner in the "ice palace". Linfield College is located in McMinnville, but we were unable to find a house that we liked in the town. However, we did find a home in Dundee, a village close to McMinnville. Our house was located on the very top of the famous "red hills of Dundee", right next to one of the many vineyards, with the most magnificent view of the north end of the Willamette Valley. We could enjoy that view from any one of thirteen sliding glass doors in the house. The house had a modern design with a very high ceiling of 26'. The house was lovely to live in the summer and the views were beautiful; but as the winter set in, ice formed on the inside of the sliding glass windows. Apparently, it was one of the coldest winters Oregon had had in a long time.

On the night of the dinner in the "ice palace", our guests were the president of Linfield, and his wife; a member of the board of trustees, and his wife; and a visiting dean from an American Baptist seminary. A snowstorm was building, when they arrived, and as the evening wore on, and as dinner was served, we found it had become so cold in the house that we couldn't sit in the dining-room and had to move down to the living-room and huddle around a wood-burning stove. As I vaguely recall, it was so cold we could see our breath and candles on the table gently wafting in response to the cold air flowing in from a nearby sliding glass door! Dorene and I were horrified at the circumstances, but there was nothing we could do; we simply could not get the house warm. And, as the wind howled and the snow swirled and the ice formed on the windows, President Walker realized that the situation had to be dealt with. So our dinner was cut short and our guests left in the middle of a blinding snowstorm, probably happy to be in the warmth of their cars as they drove back to McMinnville. Later, Dorene told me that, "We will never spend another winter in this house". And she was right—we didn't.

The snow storm turned into an ice storm as happens occasionally in the Portland area when the winds come whistling down the gorge, bringing freezing rain. So, there we were, trapped on the top of the hill with magnificent views, but the only way down in the morning was over an ice-encrusted roadway. Dorene tried to make her way down in our new car, but after traveling only a block and a half, found herself sliding out of control finally stopping a few feet away from the neighbor's swimming pool. We can now look back and laugh about it—but it wasn't a laughing matter at the time.

As spring rolled around, we finally found a house in McMinnville within walking distance of the campus. A wonderful, old, Cape Cod-style house that was one of the more pleasant homes we have ever lived in. It became a center of life for our son and his many friends. From the porch of our house, Dorene was able to watch Doug and I and his friends playing touch football in the street, an activity that went on for several years.

Living in McMinnville, small-town America, was a wonderful experience. Tom Brokaw in his autobiography details the benefits and joys of growing up in small town America: the values we cherish, the friends we make, the pace of life we follow all contribute to a general well-being felt by an entire community regardless of social class or ethnic background. The hard-working Mexican family living on one side of us was as committed to the American Dream as the DeLorean-driving physician who lived on the other side, or the golf pro and his family who lived across the street. The banker, the people who worked in the post office, the grocer, all knew their clients on a first-name basis. We all sat in the same wooden bleachers at the high school football games or at the Linfield College football games. No sky boxes, no VIP lounges, just neighbors sharing common turf.

But the move to McMinnville had a down side. Our daughter, Deborah, insisted on staying in Eugene for her senior year of high school. We felt she was mature enough to handle it, but we weren't aware of the extent to which her increased consumption of alcohol had become a way of life. The year without parental supervision deepened her addiction to the point where she drank, on and off, for the next twenty years. Until it finally killed her.

Dhaka, Bangladesh. Fall, 1984.
Dick handing out polaroid photographs to our neighbours in Dhaka.

CHAPTER 12

EXTERNAL CONSULTING AND INNER CONFLICT
(1983–1991)

AND HERE I WAS, A SUCCESSFUL EDUCATOR,
A PERSON WHO COULD ANALYZE COMPLEX SYSTEMIC
PROBLEMS FACED BY A COUNTRY,
AND I WAS UNABLE TO HELP EITHER OF MY CHILDREN
FIGHT THEIR WAY THROUGH PERSONAL ISSUES.

I've always known that I write most effectively, efficiently and passionately when writing under a deadline. Two days ago, April 24, 2006, the medical staff monitoring my case gave me the ultimate deadline: two to four weeks of living. I'll see if I can now use this pressure to complete the last two chapters of this memoir.

External Consulting

A consultant must be able to write in a clear, logical and convincing manner so that the client is able to follow the analysis and recommendations without having to ask "what is he really saying?" and "why is he saying that?" Developing this skill takes time and you need to have a thick skin. My first mentor in developing both these characteristics was Dr Lyle Fitch, the president of IPA. In 1969 I was a newly hired program officer on a project through which IPA was, in effect, providing consultant services to the United States Agency for International Development (USAID) on a number of their development projects in Africa and Latin America. The projects often entailed the development of training units that would impart knowledge and skills to government employees as part of a larger strategy to improve government efficiency and effectiveness. My job was to provide periodic assessment of progress on these projects and write a quarterly report. I'll never forget Lyle's comments on my first draft report. It came back to me with more red ink than black ink. I was devastated. When Dr Mark Cannon (Ph.D. Harvard), my immediate superior and destined to become the first administrative assistant to the chief of the United States supreme court, saw the shock on my face, he comforted me by saying that his first draft from Lyle had been covered in even more red.

My problem was due, in part, to the fact that I had unconsciously adopted the writing style of Max Weber, Talcott Parsons and Fred Riggs, scholars whose work I had focused on in my Ph.D. studies. Students of public administration and political science know that these three are noted for their complex writing. For example, Parsons is known for having single sentences almost a page in length. But

Lyle Fitch shocked me into becoming an effective writer and analyst, so that by the time I was pursuing more consulting activities as a faculty member at the University of Oregon, my abilities to listen, analyze and write effective reports were an asset.

My commitment to the value of "learning from experience" which had begun at Gravers School, reinforced my efforts to balance my teaching role with consulting activities, in the expectation that the lessons gained from consulting would inform my teaching, and the knowledge and skill gained from research would inform my consulting skills. Many academics with consulting practices keep their key roles in "separate compartments". The consulting compartment is the smaller of the two and is often driven by a need to earn supplementary income rather than as a source of continued professional development of knowledge and skills. Separation rather than integration was more often the consequence of institutional policies regarding the declaring of outside income by academics. But for Jim Marshall, my first consulting partner, and myself, it was about the integration of the learning from consulting into our teaching roles that was a driving motivator for our small practice. And, whenever we could, we involved students in our consulting activities so that they could develop an appreciation of the cycle of experience (consulting) in informing teaching and research, leading to better skills and analysis, and a more nuanced understanding of the limitations and applicability of theories in the real world.

The first major consultancy that Jim Marshall and I had was with a group of federal, state, county, city and voluntary agencies in Lincoln County, Oregon, in 1975. The clients of these agencies were welfare recipients, and our task was to try to systematize inter-agency co-ordination in order to minimize the chances of clients "falling through the cracks". We identified a number of issues that prevented better co-ordination, for example, misunderstood policies on confidentiality had limited what information caseworkers from one agency felt they could share with caseworkers from another. The fact that the offices of different agencies were physically apart made it difficult for clients and caseworkers to get together and co-ordinate their activities. And, finally, the absence of head caseworkers meant that no one was in charge or an advocate of a particular case.

Borrowing from Robert Persig's analysis of gumption robbing

factors in his best-selling book *Zen and the Art of Motorcycle Maintenance*, we recommended a set of innovative actions that put gumption back into the system rather than sucking it out. Our clients championed these recommendations with their policy-makers and ultimately won approval for their implementation. A key example of an accepted recommendation that had a fundamental impact on co-ordination was the development of a single building in which all of the welfare activities of these agencies were located. It was the first time in the state of Oregon that such a simple approach to co-ordination had been undertaken, and its effect was an immediate improvement of co-ordination between agencies and a much more client-sensitive service to welfare recipients. Rather than shuttling from one building to another, often on foot and with small children in tow in Oregon's rainy weather, they came to one facility, with a child-care service, and were able to conduct their business in "one stop".

Probably the most important lesson we learned from our three-year project in Lincoln County was how critical it was to establish an active communication process between our clients and ourselves. Establishing such a process became a central feature of my approach to consulting and, through the rigorous use of highly iterative communication, gave me the courage to make a major change— a paradigm shift in my consulting. Yvonna Lincoln and Evon Guba were the seminal writers on the paradigm shift from "third generation" to "fourth generation" evaluation. Most consultants, knowingly or unknowingly, operate from the third generation model of evaluation, which assumes the consultant to be an objective, impartial expert whose expertise will guide the client to solutions for problems. The fourth generation rejects most of these assumptions, starting with the notion of objectivity and impartiality. Consultants are seldom objective because reality is seldom objective. Ask any cop who has interviewed ten eye witnesses and they will tell you they have heard ten different representations of reality. So the role of the consultant in fourth generation evaluation becomes more of a guide to finding the most commonly accepted definition of the problem and then the most acceptable path to a solution. All of which makes the role of iterative communication essential for the implementation of solutions. A fundamental problem with third generation consultancies is that the consultant studies the situation, interviews a few relevant people, then writes the report and leaves. The commitment to implementing recommendations is assumed—an assumption that is frequently wrong. As a consequence, most consultant reports become additions to someone's bookcase, the findings and recommendations rapidly fading into distant memories, while the situation that brought the consultant into the picture remains alive and dysfunctional.

In fourth generation work, the consultant spends a great deal of time negotiating an implementation plan that all parties agree to, with clear assignments, time lines and accountability. The consultant's report becomes a dog-eared document, never far from the reach of clients, and the consultant is often expected to return to the situation to monitor what is taking place.

This is clearly a "messier" process—but it works, it creates results, and that's the difference.

This is a gross simplification of the fourth generation model. I've written elsewhere in greater detail about my first formal application of it and the evaluation of a USAID Human Resource Development project in Malawi in 1990. My point in discussing it has been to illustrate the on-going process of learning from experience and growth, and the evolution in my approach to consulting. During the 1970s, while at the University of Oregon, I was involved in approximately a dozen major consultancies, some as long as four years, some as short as one month. Most were focused on clients in Oregon, though two were for international clients involving work in Liberia and Mexico. While dean at Linfield, I was expected to focus entirely on the administrative responsibilities of building new programs, so during that five-year period my consulting work dried up. Consequently, when I was invited by the American University to be the senior human resource consultant on a World Bank project in Bangladesh, I seized the opportunity because it opened the way back into international consulting at a fairly significant level.

The Bangladesh project was designed to be a failure; not intentionally, but that was the outcome. The government of Bangladesh didn't want the project but needed to accept it in order to have access to other World Bank funds. The World Bank wanted it but it was designed with a deaf ear to how the Bangladeshis thought it might be made somewhat more useful. Professionally, involvement in this year-long project, living in Bangladesh, was probably the worst experience of my life. Personally, living in Bangladesh was "interesting and challenging". Dorene would stand by the window of our apartment for hours wondering what in the world we were doing there, as she watched Bengali women smashing bricks with a hammer all day long in order to make gravel for concrete that was being used to pave the street in front of our complex. In the days before the Internet, to make an international call, you needed to book it a week in advance. Fax services were unreliable, so good, old fashioned "snail mail" was the most effective means of communication and we have a box or more of carbon copies of the letters that Dorene wrote to friends that long year. We met some amazing Bengalis who struggled for independence on both a personal and national level. We traveled to India, Nepal and Thailand in order to find relief from the poverty of Dhaka. After a year in Bangladesh we returned home and I enthusiastically pursued new international consulting opportunities.

Between 1984 and 1991, I was involved in more than twenty consultancies in a wide range of countries including India, Pakistan, back to Bangladesh, Indonesia, Nepal, Egypt, Malawi, Zimbabwe, Ecuador, Honduras and Costa Rica. I returned to a number of these countries on several different consulting assignments. My clients were either USAID, the World Bank or the United Nations Development Program. The nature of the consultancies ranged from evaluating an on-going activity to designing new programs which the client was likely to fund. As mentioned in earlier comments, I favored design activities over evaluation activities because they created an opportunity for innovation and the synthesis of a variety of new approaches. In evaluation one was simply seeing the extent to which somebody else's design was being implemented. In most of the consultancies I was a part of a team of professionals brought in to carry out the work, mostly as the team leader, which put the onus on me to integrate different disciplinary viewpoints into an effective frame of action. And, it often meant that I would be writing the final report late into the night in order to meet the time lines. In part that's where the ability to produce under tight deadlines was honed.

The content of these consultancies ranged from the strengthening of local government to the redesign of higher-education systems and the building of training capacity in order to improve the management of government agencies. But regardless of the content, the process of developing a relationship with the agencies (that were either the clients or the intended beneficiaries of donor activities) followed a process of much interaction and discussion before providing an analysis of the problem or recommended plan of action. This was the signature characteristic of the consultancies I was involved with. Initially, some of my consulting colleagues were put off by the prospect of going back to that same agency two or three times and listening to what other agencies were saying, either about the definition of the problem or some recommended changes. But once they got "the picture", once they recognized how critically important having a shared perception of reality was in determining the likely success of either an evaluation or a design, they began accepting the approach. I suspect that a number of them left with a revised understanding of their own objectivity and became more honest in acknowledging that subjective reality is, by and large, the main reality experience.

Internal Conflicts (1986–2006)

As I reflect on what I've written about my years as a consultant, what I've failed to illuminate is the fact that I was not only a practicing professional, but also a member of a family with family responsibilities, with our own sets of issues and dynamics, and with plans and dreams that we sought to achieve together. This is necessary to give a more balanced view of my world between 1983 and 1991. But as Dorene points out, my traveling primarily took place after our children were grown up. On many occasions, she traveled with me. In the periods that I was home, I was involved in remodeling our houses as we moved from one to another; doing the kinds of things we expect of fathers and husbands nowadays. So, it wasn't all a narrow focus on professional growth and development, on filling several passports with enough diverse entries to raise eyebrows at immigration control, both in the US and in the many countries visited. I also tried to learn from the experiences of our family and other families in addressing some of the issues and realities we were facing during that same period.

The principal reality was our growing awareness that both our daughter and son "were using". Our daughter's case was the more extreme. She cycled through productive periods then would slowly lose control and lapse back into a pattern of alcohol abuse and bulimia. Deborah was an intelligent and strikingly beautiful woman—the latter fact she never learned to live with comfortably. Her beauty and her vulnerability attracted men, adding pressure to find ways to respond. She kept us at arms' length when she actually needed us the most. The conflict Dorene and I were experiencing in trying to deal with her situation was heightened by the conflicting guidance from counseling professionals, beginning in her early teen years. Some told us this was just a phase, and we should "back off". Others told us to treat her with "tough love"; later, others said we should worry about ourselves—Deborah needed to face her own reality. Dorene recognized worrisome patterns which prompted professional counseling. She alerted Deborah to the alcohol problems in Deborah's grandparents' generation, but we didn't learn for some time that alcoholism could actually "skip" a generation. And had. It really didn't matter that we'd moved from the bad influences of DC to what we thought was a more wholesome environment in Eugene, Oregon.

In the meantime our son graduated from high school and then did nothing, at least nothing constructive that indicated he had a direction or a sense of life's purpose. Like his sister, he started community college several times, but never completed a course. And here I was, a successful educator, a person who could analyze complex systemic problems faced by a country, and I was unable to help either of my children fight their way through personal issues.

Both went through residential treatment programs without being able to make lasting changes in behavior. Both cycled through jobs, staying long enough to build a little equity to support their respective habits. Sometimes they lived at home, but that only briefly moderated their bad habits.

Finally, in 1984 the situation with Deborah reached another crisis. We intervened as her family and she headed off to one of Minnesota's well-known drug treatment programs. She did well, stayed there, found a job and fell in love with a young man, Jim Jester, who was also an alumnus of a recovery program in Minneapolis. They married and moved back to Oregon, living in a cottage on our property in McMinnville. In March 1986 our granddaughter, Dara Alexis Jester, was born and Deborah entered a period of successful mothering, enjoying tranquility for several years.

In the meantime, Doug's situation went from bad to worse. An intervention saw him on his way to Minneapolis. A week later, after an attempted suicide, he was back in Oregon. Over the next few years Doug was in and out of treatment programs, halfway houses, and spent countless nights sleeping on the floors of friends. Denial was Doug's subjective reality and nothing we could say or do could alter that.

By 1989 Deborah's reality was also changing. She had re-established contact with Curtis Bosworth, the first true love of her life. Her decision to divorce Jim, move to California to be with Curtis and ultimately remarry, drove Jim "off the wagon" and our precious granddaughter became a full-time presence in our lives. His drug of choice had been heroin, and he went back to it. The months ahead were cliffhangers for us. It was like the worst soap opera, and it was happening to us. I was trying to keep us afloat through my peripatetic consulting work. Dorene miraculously kept her sanity, focusing all her energy on raising our granddaughter, Dara, then three years old.

Deborah and Curtis married and moved back to Portland from California. Dara was reunited with her mother. Jim was hanging onto reality by his fingertips. Doug was still floating, detached from reality. By 1991 Deborah's life seemed stable, and Dorene and I left for South Africa. But slowly, as the months and years ticked by, she lost control again. She and Curtis divorced, and Doug, who had settled down with his partner, Roberta, and had a job, moved in with Deborah and Dara to help share costs.

Over the next few years we arranged for Deborah and Dara to visit us in Johannesburg and Dorene and I made frequent trips home to Portland. A pretense of normality settled over our family until June 5, 1998. On that day Dorene and I returned from an overnight safari north of Johannesburg. As we entered our house around 6 p.m. I saw the answering machine was blinking. It was our dear friend,

Walt Ellis, calling us to tell us that Deborah was in hospital, on life support. Her heart had suddenly stopped functioning while she was in the process of checking into the hospital. My first utterance to Dorene was "our world has changed forever". Walt encouraged us to head home immediately. The last flight out of Johannesburg was at 10 in the evening. A quick call secured us the last two seats. I then realized we didn't have our passports. I had turned them in several days earlier to have additional pages added. While I tracked down someone at the US consulate who could issue us temporary travel documents, Dorene was scrambling to pack and close up the house. A Ford Foundation colleague, Alice Brown, raced us to the consulate, and then the airport. We arrived with five minutes to spare. The flight to Portland was a blur, but time stopped when we walked into the ICU at St Vincent's Hospital. Nothing can prepare a parent for a moment like that. There was nothing that could be done. She was already brain dead. We simply had to formalize the only option. We left her on life support for the night so Dorene and I could spend time with her.

In the morning all Deborah's family and friends gathered to say goodbye. We sang Amazing Grace and then the life support was turned off, and it was over. But it wasn't; it isn't; it won't ever be. The inner conflict may have lost its sharp edges, but it is still there.

Deborah's death was a wake-up call for Doug; his life has been straight and stable since then. He has a steady job which he loves; he and Roberta have been blessed with a wonderful son, Wyatt Richard, born September 30, 2003, who will help fill up the hole in Dorene's heart when I am gone. Dara Alexis is excelling in college, a level-headed young woman with a clear sense of who she is and where she is going. Her father continues to be part of our lives; and Curtis Bosworth and his young family have become part of our perfectly modern, extended family.

Chapter 13

The South African Years
(1991–2000)

I WAS SEEN NOT SO MUCH AS AN EXTERNAL
MONITOR CHECKING UP ON HOW THE GRANTEES
WERE SPENDING THEIR MONEY, BUT MORE AS A
PARTNER IN BRINGING ABOUT THE CHANGE
WE ALL SOUGHT.

1999.
Alice Brown, currently Ford Foundation representative in South Africa, and Dick at his farewell party.

The decade Dorene and I lived in South Africa, was, without doubt, the highlight of our lives— from my perspective at least. To say that we developed an intense emotional relationship with the country and the many friends and colleagues we gained during that decade is an understatement. It's a challenge to unbundle these feelings and identify the reasons for them.

The reasons for our passionate love would certainly include the following: a strong affinity for the democratic ideals the country was pursuing and for the incredibly transparent process it was following in pursuit of these ideals; a strong affinity for the country's radical transformation regarding the value of diversity from apartheid in its ugliest form to a democratic, non-racist, non-sexist society; the pure excitement of being witness to and part of the rebirth of a nation, a rebirth hailed by the world's press and world's leaders as "the miracle" of the 20th century; the open, honest, sincerity of South Africans of all racial/ethnic groups and their ability to look at themselves and their past with a sense of humor, a sense of forgiveness and a commitment to "getting it right" this time. And, finally, the absolute beauty of the country, from the rugged beauty of the Drakensberg mountains and the Wild Coast to the majesty of Table Mountain and the peculiar beauty of the Karoo.

We went to South Africa in 1991. I was on a one-year assignment as a management development specialist, one of a three-person team through Creative Associates International, a DC-based consulting firm. Creative had a contract with USAID South Africa to begin developing black leadership in selected sectors. The years of apartheid had stifled black leadership development, yet it was inevitable that change was coming. To facilitate these changes many African Americans headed to South Africa driven by an obligation to help their black brothers and sisters forge a peaceful way forward. The expectations of African Americans were far beyond what they were likely to realize. In many cases this led to bitterness and a sense of rejection, but mostly a sense of confusion.

Conversely, white Americans, myself included, came with relatively little expectations. We knew that our government had been party to the support of the apartheid state and as we were there representing the US government through a USAID contract, there was no reason for us to expect that we would be welcomed with open arms. To make progress, we would have to show prudence and careful commitment, and deliver promises on time and in a form which was in response to the demands of black South Africans. The day after I arrived I was met by a white South African woman, one of the leaders of a women's peace movement in South Africa. She took me to her upscale, northern Johannesburg residence for lunch where she provided me with a quick briefing of what to do and what not to do. I shall never forget her firm words of advice, "don't be a typical American who gets off the plane and begins to tell us what to do; sit here for a couple of months with your mouth shut and listen and observe and only then can you begin to tentatively make suggestions about ways to move forward". There was nothing malicious in the way she said it, it was all well intended and it was all well received.

My methodology as a consultant, learning to rely upon the importance of developing a shared perception of reality, reinforced my need to understand first and foremost the perception of reality that white and black South Africans had of their way forward and of the role that organizations, like USAID, with a deeply flawed political past may or may not be able to play. My role was to work with the higher-education sector, but because the apartheid regime was still in power we could not work directly with South Africa's universities and technikons (technical colleges), since they were all, legally, creatures of the state. Under the guidelines of the Congressional Anti-Apartheid Act passed by the US Congress years ago, no South African state organization could receive any US government funds, so my job was to find NGOs working in and with universities and technikons, and design activities that would build black leadership capacity in these organizations.

Before leaving for South Africa in July of 1991, our three-person team was briefed by Ambassador Perkins. He had been appointed US ambassador to South Africa when Reagan was president and his appointment was controversial, to say the least, since he was an African American. But he was also, first and foremost, a professional diplomat, so he managed the situation well despite the discomfort he caused the South African government.

The most important gem of wisdom Ambassador Perkins gave us in our briefing was that when apartheid fell we should not assume that South African's black universities and technikons would be effective instruments of change. Since they were created by the apartheid government, they were viewed by many blacks as illegitimate. His wisdom has been borne out many times, yet it was wisdom that foreign donors, including USAID, failed to accept as they sought to pour millions of dollars into the black institutions. When Professor Kader Asmal became the second minister of education under South Africa's post-apartheid government, he moved aggressively to "deconstruct" these institutions through mergers with white institutions. Professor Asmal had been a leading academic at South Africa's premier black university, the University of the Western Cape. Yet the illegitimacy of these institutions was an important factor in his plan for restructuring South African higher education in 1999.

In 1992, after one year, Creative's contract with USAID was extended and I was privileged to be able to stay on another year. In the early 1990s USAID made a determination that its support for education in a post-apartheid South Africa needed to be focused since it didn't have the budget resources to be effective across the entire sector and it began to narrow its focus to higher education and adult basic education, which is why I had been tasked to focus on identifying NGOs in those two areas and to link them with activities that were under way. Over the first two years that I was there I attended dozens of meetings called by the ANC education desk, aimed at identifying activities needed to correct the state of affairs in South African higher education and in adult basic education. The latter focus put me in contact with many of the people working on the ANC labor side, where labor was seen as a vehicle for addressing adult basic education needs. These connections became quite important as I sought in later years to support efforts by South African universities and technikons to develop programming that might address the on-going needs of people in the labor force for continued professional development.

I mentioned that I developed an intense emotional relationship with South Africa partly because of a deep appreciation for the incredibly transparent process South Africans used to tear down apartheid. This process was worth noting because of the power it gave to the efforts to bring about change. As I indicated, I attended dozens of meetings where issues concerning change were discussed. Many of those meetings were meetings where just ANC members or members of a broader liberation constituency were present. But many of the meetings were meetings that had representatives of the government as well as members of the ANC present. What characterized the nature of these meetings was the adherence to procedural rules that assured speakers ample time to make their point and it assured listeners ample time to address the points made. Meetings were always conducted with utmost regard for following rules of order. Civility was a requirement and everybody knew and understood this because underlying whatever was being said there was a palpable tension brought about by the remembrances of injustices, inequities and, often times, of pain and suffering to those present or to family members of those present. Yet through it all, I never attended a meeting where things got out of hand. If they showed signs of reaching that point, the chair always called for a break, and always encouraged caucuses of various groups during the break in order to permit them to refocus on the issues and to bring their emotions under control.

The best run meetings I have ever witnessed in my life were meetings run by either ANC officials or South African government officials where the issues were laden with emotion, where the stakes were high but where the commitment to civility and transparency were clearly observed in order to make progress. Perhaps this inherent trait of civility could be traced to indigenous tribal tradition where tribal elders sought to hear all sides of an issue and calmly debated matters and administered justice in the cool and tranquil shade of the largest tree in the village. After retiring and returning to Portland I was elected president of our homeowner's association. On many occasions I found myself making the sad comparison between the orderly conduct of meetings in South Africa, where the issues at stake were much higher, and the raucous, impolite behavior of some of our homeowners in our annual meetings; comparing the rude exchanges between homeowners with petty gripes to meetings in South Africa where ANC members were able to conduct their business in a civil and progressive manner even though their family members had suffered viciously at the hands of government officials with whom they were now meeting. This comparison raises and answers the question as to where democracy was working best.

Anyone who watched the multi-party negotiations under way at the World Trade Center in Johannesburg in 1993 will clearly remember the decorum that allowed those talks to go on despite the nature of the grievances that were being discussed. It was a model of how meetings should be run and it was broadcast live on television so that the rank and file could see not only what their leaders were saying but how they were behaving.

No one will ever forget that dramatic evening when F.W. de Klerk, as the spokesperson for the government, crossed the line in criticizing the ANC and its terrorist activities. The world watched with baited breath as Nelson Mandela, obviously angered as no one had seen him angered before, strode to the microphone to respond to the government. This was a moment at which the talks could have broken down. It was a moment in which justifiable anger on the part of the ANC through the voice of Nelson Mandela, could have led the delegates on a walkout and scuttled the process. Rather, the nation watched transfixed, as Mandela, his voice at times choking with emotion, rejected the charges of the government and laid out the ANC's rationale for the necessity of subversive activities in order to throw off the yoke of apartheid. When he finished speaking, there was no doubt that he had made his points forcefully, dramatically and with a degree of finality that left the government with nothing more to say and that all that was left to do was to continue onward with the talks, which they did.

I began focusing some of my attention on the higher education sector and, on an occasion in 1991 or early 1992, I attended a conference at the University of the Witwatersrand (Wits) where the president of South Africa's Human Sciences Research Council (HSRC), one of the seven statutory research bodies, established, funded and operated by the South African government (although they were supposedly independent) was seeking to engage the higher education community to discuss common research interests and agendas. The HSRC was a major source of funding to South African universities for research in the education sector, among other areas, but its grants generally went to Afrikaans universities. Making a gesture to Wits, an English-speaking university and one with a long history of protest against apartheid, the HSRC was trying to signal a more even handed approach to the awarding of grants for research.

Several hundred people were there and when the HSRC president had finished his remarks, and the floor was opened for questions and comments, I was struck by the aggressive questioning that came from one, young, white Afrikaner, employed at Wits in the student-counseling center. His background was in psychology and he had been a student of the president of the HSRC when he was a senior faculty member at a South African university. The questioner had a thick Afrikaans accent and prefaced his remarks with the disclaimer, as it were, that while the president of the HSRC had been the chairman of his dissertation committee, the questioner felt no obligation to be humble or respectful of the earlier connection. Rather the questioner went on, asking how someone with the intelligence of the speaker could have the audacity to come forward representing what was clearly the mouthpiece for apartheid South Africa's education research and seek to engage the anti-apartheid education activists.

The brash, even aggressive, questioning, and its underlying humor, mostly at the expense of the president of the HSRC, made an impression on me. Afterwards, I was told he was Dr Nico Cloete and that, among other things, he was the general secretary of a national union of academics from most of South Africa's universities, the Union of Democratic University Staff Associations (UDUSA). This was precisely the kind of organization that USAID wanted to support, so I asked Nico for a meeting.

He came to that meeting extremely suspicious at my motivations and started off by asking if I was a "fucking CIA agent". Interestingly my family had been asking me that question for years when I kept showing up in so-called "hot spots" around the world, such as Chile, Pakistan, Bangladesh, Honduras and other places. But I assured him, as I had assured my family, that I was not a CIA agent and had never, to my knowledge, even talked with any CIA agents. Our conversation continued and I explained my role and asked Nico what sort of support UDUSA might find useful in helping to forward its agenda. He came back to me a couple of days later with an extremely modest proposal. I used that proposal to begin to put us on a common footing and asked him what sort of "shit activity" he was proposing because there was no viable way the proposal could have the kind of impact UDUSA was trying to make. Nico was taken aback somewhat by my manner and also by the fact that I was so straightforward in criticizing what he had proposed. Many of the NGOs who received donor support from around the world were not used to criticism. They were used to open wallets and unquestioning support for their activities. Apparently I was different, so several days later Nico came back with a much more thoughtful and comprehensive proposal.

That was the beginning of a personal and professional relationship that has lasted more than fifteen years. Nico represented, and continues to represent, the sharp, independent, analytic approach, born in the cauldrons of protest, fully capable of aggressively dismembering ideas that are not grounded in the realities and best thinking of the day.

It was through people like Nico that my intellectual commitment to South Africa deepened, but it was also through the connections with people like Ann and Austin Evans that we were emotionally awakened to the bright future that South Africa was pursuing. Ann and Austin were our "landlords" and over the years we spent thousands of hours in each other's company as they introduced us to a side of South Africa that my professional work had no access to. One of our early Christmases in South Africa, we shared a rented house in Constantia with the Evans' family, deepening our knowledge of South Africa's wonderful wines. Of course that meant having to visit the vineyards of the Western Cape but it was a chore we managed to struggle through.

After the death of our daughter in 1998 and our return to South Africa, Ann was the one who could take me aside, grab my hands and look deeply into my eyes and insist upon knowing how I was *really* handling the situation. Ann and Austin also helped us to identify places to go on our monthly weekends away from Johannesburg, exploring the wonderful bed and breakfast world of South Africa. In fact, we quickly reached the point where we were sharing our new finds with them as well as others, such as John and Meryn Turner's bed and breakfast at Babanango. John Turner's wonderfully detailed description of the events of the day on his guided tour of Isandlwana and Rorke's Drift, deepened our understanding of the history between South Africa's largest indigenous tribal group, the

Zulus, and the British colonials, whose stupidity at times seemed boundless.

Actually, I spent my first Christmas in Johannesburg in 1991 while Dorene went home to spend time with family. During the 1991 Christmas break Jonathan Jansen invited me to accompany him and his family home to Cape Town. He and his friends took me on my first hike up and across Table Mountain, introducing me to some of the most spectacular views to be found anywhere in the world. I stayed with a friend of Jonathan's in the suburb of Cape Town called Observatory. My host was Damian Ruth and over the years, Damian, Dorene and I shared many wonderful times together in Observatory and in Johannesburg, discussing the future of the country and the journey its political leaders were navigating.

In 1993, when it became clear that the apartheid government was going to end sooner rather than later, the Ford Foundation decided to open an office in Johannesburg. The Ford Foundation had been a major supporter of efforts since the mid-1980s to help the white, English-speaking universities of South Africa—namely, the University of Cape Town, Wits University, the University of Natal and Rhodes University—to develop programs for black students and academic staff. These efforts, and programs in other fields such as human rights, support for the arts, and support for black leadership development in the judicial system and other democratic institutions, were all run through Ford's New York office. This was not a desirable way to operate programs, but it was the only option at the time. So, when it became clear that a democratic election would be held in 1994 and a new government would be in place, Ford moved aggressively to open an office in Johannesburg.

One of the four program officer positions was to be an education program officer, someone with a thorough understanding of the issues confronting South African higher education, and someone who would be acceptable to the ANC. When my name was put forward by John Gerhart, the representative of the Ford Foundation in South Africa, to John Samuel of the ANC's education desk, there was a positive response. When I was offered the position I accepted and began what was the most rewarding job I have ever held, working with the best people I have ever been privileged to work with, including colleagues at Ford and "grantees" of the foundation.

When I retired from Ford in 2000, I was able to maintain both sets of associations through the research and publications I now had the time to pursue. These activities brought us back to South Africa on a regular basis through to 2004. And while the love affair with South Africa has moved into a different phase, it has not lost any of its intensity.

It should be noted that John Gerhart and his wife, Gail, who is a professor at Columbia University, had a long and deep connection to South Africa. Gail and her research partner, Tom Karras, had interviewed all of the liberation movement leaders as well as rank and file members on several occasions leading to the publication of seven volumes on the history of the movement and the roles played by the thousands of individuals who took part in it. In John Gerhart's twenty years of work at the Ford Foundation, he was often in a position to make sure that proposals from South Africa were well received and funded. John Samuel and John Gerhart were old friends and had a deep mutual respect for each other's wisdom and a deep connection to ANC education-related activities.

That I was able to stay in South Africa was in large measure due to the approval I had gained from the ANC's education desk in the person of John Samuel for the work that I had been doing on the Creative Associates (CA) project and in some related activities. John's voice was incredibly important on all matters related to education. No donor undertook any activities aimed at supporting anti-apartheid activities in the area of education, without routing their intentions, their plans and their support through John Samuel.

There's an interesting story about some work that I did in the second year of my CA contract for the World Bank. The World Bank was interested in helping the ANC determine what the management needs would be of a new department of education in post-apartheid South Africa, so steps could be taken to prepare people to fill the various roles. One day some World Bank people showed up and asked me if I was interested in conducting such a study for them. I suspect David Evans of USAID, with whom I had been working closely on some other studies in the education sector, had also pointed them in my direction. In any case, they outlined what the study would look like. I listened politely and then told them that I wasn't interested because it didn't seem feasible that one person, a non-

South African, who had had very little contact with the apartheid government's department of education, would be able to carry out the study with any validity. They acted surprised. Generally people didn't turn down the World Bank when asked to carry out a study. So they asked me what I thought was needed. I said I thought this required more than one person: a team of four or five people, all South Africans, all of whom were familiar with the operations of the many departments of education even though they were opposed to the current government's apartheid education policies and programs. We negotiated a little more, and they left saying they needed to think about it. I suspect thinking about it meant going back to John Samuel and seeing what he thought, and I can imagine John sitting there smiling in his inimitable way, amused at the idea of someone telling the World Bank that they had a half-baked idea. In any event, I think he must have concurred because they came back to me and said, "Okay, we think your idea is good, let's talk about additional people." The end result was that I had a team of four South Africans, who were exceptionally well informed about how apartheid worked, financially, politically and, to some extent, with regards to education.

The team we assembled included Professor Jonathan Jansen, a black South African who had worked with me two years previously on an evaluation of a USAID education project in Zimbabwe and with whom I currently shared office space in Johannesburg. It also included Mary Metcalf, a stalwart in ANC education circles and a person with a deep understanding of the political machinations of the apartheid government's education activities. Among other things, Mary had been a teacher in Soweto and was on the teaching staff of the Johannesburg College of Education. A white South African, she was among the forefront of ANC members destined to have a bigger impact on reshaping South Africa's education efforts when the ANC took over. The third member of the team was Peter Buckland, an education policy analyst at the Urban Foundation, a largely white think-tank focusing on education and urban affairs matters, and highly critical of the apartheid government. Peter had spent time in departments of education in the so-called "Homelands" so he was familiar with the operations of those organizations. And, the final member of the team, Zeph Senkane, the rector of a black teacher training college who also was thoroughly familiar with the operations of the current South African government.

As a team we interviewed top education-department officials in eighteen of the nineteen departments of education in South Africa. The mere fact that there were nineteen departments of education indicates the bizarre consequences of an apartheid approach to what should be a fairly straightforward, unified field of government activity. Each of the four historical provinces had a white department of education, there was a department of education for each of the so-called "Homelands" or independent territories, a department of education serving South Africa's Indian population, a department of education and training serving black South Africans who didn't live in the homelands, but lived in one of the four provinces. And then there was an overall co-ordinating department of education. In our interviews with the top department officials in each of these departments, we asked them what they anticipated might occur under a post-apartheid South Africa and what those changes implied in terms of new staffing and new management needs.

Our study was well received by the World Bank and the ANC education desk for a number of reasons, but mostly importantly because it was a breakthrough. It was the first time that anyone outside the current government had made a systematic effort to anticipate the impact of changes, not just on the schools and on the teachers, but on the management of this new undertaking from a policy point of view. One of the more interesting and perhaps controversial findings of our study was our declaration that the most efficient department of education among the nineteen was the department that served South Africa's Indian population. It produced more graduates, that is, a higher percentage of the students it served graduated from high school than any other department, yet it did so at a cost per student that was not as high as that realized in the white departments. So, our finding of the department of education for Indian Affairs as the most efficient made headlines and, again, I can see John Samuel smiling as he read this. John, of an Indian background himself, probably knew all along that the department was the best but it was unthinkable in those days for anyone to suggest anything was more efficient than the white departments.

When I joined the Ford Foundation, John Gerhart became

my mentor and guide regarding our deepening knowledge and appreciation of all things South African, particularly in the area of the arts. John was a collector and an expert. Every time he headed out to the Soweto Art Gallery, or his favorite arts and crafts shop, he would invite me along. And when he had extra tickets to the Market Theatre—South Africa's premier venue for theatre: the only place where protest plays had been performed during the dark days of apartheid and the only place where black and white people could perform and even sit together—Dorene and I were the beneficiaries of those tickets. Our love for the country was intensified by South Africa's art community, which had been enriched by black artists whose work had long been unrecognized.

Many of my South African friends recognized the extent of my patriotic feelings towards South Africa. This was made poignantly clear when I travelled with a group of South African higher-education leaders to a meeting in Washington, DC. As we entered immigration control at JFK, I split from the group to get in the US citizens' line. As I passed my fellow travelers, Njabulo Ndbele, vice chancellor of the University of Cape Town said, "Dick, it's so strange seeing you over there, you really belong here with us." Fortunately my line turned away at that point, and I was able to conceal my tears from them. The ultimate tribute, it touched me profoundly.

It also revealed how intensely my love affair with South Africa had grown. Serving one-year contracts in 1991 and 1992, I had been reluctant to make an emotional commitment to South Africa despite having done so on an intellectual level. But with the Ford Foundation appointment, I was assured of having at least three more years in South Africa, so both Dorene and I followed our hearts into the new, for us, heartland of Africa.

A primary consequence of becoming a Ford Foundation program officer was that I had a budget to work with: a pool of money that could be used to support the activities of the South African organizations I recommended. The Foundation's approval of my recommendations was quick and reliable. It was a much more satisfactory relationship than with USAID. Therefore it wasn't surprising that the opportunities for my greater involvement in developing an agenda for South African higher-education policy reform became much more substantial. For example, I was appointed to the ANC's Higher Education Task Force, one of a number of task forces set up to prepare for what might happen when a new government came into being.

The Higher Education Task Force had five members: Dr Teboho Moja who was the presiding president of UDUSA and an emerging, articulate, informed voice about higher education matters; Nico Cloete; Rob Segal, an Australian who had immigrated to South Africa and was deeply involved in efforts to make white universities more accessible to black students; and Harold Wolpe, a distinguished academic who had recently returned from exile and was one of John Samuels' trusted inner circle. Harold and his wife, AnnMarie, were important historical figures in the fight against apartheid. In 1963 Harold had been arrested by the South African police for acts of treason and was sentenced to years in prison, but he and his co-defendant managed to escape and were the subject of the then largest man-hunt in South African history. AnnMarie recounts this experience in thrilling detail as well as their escape to London and their eventual return to South Africa in 1990 in her book, *The Long Way Home*.

I digress: I was appointed by John Samuel to the Higher Education Task Force and our job was to prepare an action agenda concerning higher education for the minister of education after the ANC took over the government. First and foremost on our agenda was the recommendation for a proclamation establishing a national commission on higher education which would make a thorough study of the sector and make necessary policy-change recommendations. The drafts of the Higher Education Task Force report, and of the actual presidential proclamation, were done on my laptop. When Nelson Mandela became president in 1994, his very first presidential proclamation was the creation of a National Commission on Higher Education, just as we had recommended. Dr Jairam Reddy, the vice-chancellor of The University of Durban-Westville, chaired the commission. Teboho Moja was named executive director, Nico Cloete became the research director and Harold Wolpe the chair of the commission's most important working group. However, I stayed in the background and through the Ford Foundation became one of the commission's sources of funding.

My general funding strategy in the early years of my role as program officer, was to try to get South Africa's universities and technikons, forced to work in isolation under apartheid, to begin working together to overcome historical disparities and isolation. For example, we funded the development of five regional consortia of institutions. These consortia became useful round tables for senior university officials around which to share ideas and plans, and for staff and faculty at departmental level to plan and implement joint activities.

Another funding objective was to strengthen the National Association of Development Officers (UNITECH) at universities and technikons so that pursuing funds might become more collaborative rather than competitive, and that the historically white universities with strong development offices might be able to assist black institutions to build capacity and develop professionalism in their own development offices.

Other activities included supporting black institutions in developing capacity to do strategic planning, both individually and collectively, in order to catch up with the white institutions, all of which had strong strategic planning units and were moving forward aggressively to enhance their capability for attracting funds and students.

A fourth strategic line of funding was to support the South African Institute for Distance Education and its efforts to help interested institutions develop high-quality distance education and open learning programs. Although South Africa had the world's largest distance university, UNISA, as well as a distance education technikon, both of these institutions were so closely aligned with the previous government that their work was regularly compromised by politically incorrect curricula as well as by staff who often did not share a commitment to the educational ideas espoused by the new South African government.

The most important of our funding strategies in the early years was the creation of a higher education policy think-tank that would continue the work started by the National Commission. Since the commission was a temporary effort, it was clear that South Africa would need, for a long time to come, a think-tank that could focus on refreshing the agenda for policy reform, reviewing and evaluating policy efforts that had been implemented, convening constructive debate and promoting networking with higher education policy analysts around the world. This think-tank became the Centre for Higher Education Transformation (CHET) with Dr Nico Cloete as its director.

It is instructive to reflect on the transformation programs I was involved with as a program officer for the Ford Foundation in South Africa in contrast to programs in many consultancies around the world. Significantly, I was available at all times to respond to and work with grantees as they developed their proposals and then, once funded through a grant, went on to implement the activities. The mere fact of being able to engage in an on-going conversation, aware of subtle shifts and perceptions of reality, made it more likely that the changes had been justified and supported by the grantee.

The second major difference was that I was seen not so much as an external monitor checking up on how the grantees were spending their money, but more as a partner in bringing about the change we all sought. That degree of integration seldom occurs in the typical situation, yet it is vital for ensuring that the consultant's and the client's visions are shared, not only of the outcomes, but also of the process of achieving them.

When we decided on a justifiable need to change direction in a South African undertaking, we were able to change direction without a big fuss. There was one thing the grantees had to learn about our programs, however. Many South African NGOs had received donor support for years from various international organizations with very few strings attached and with little expectation of accountability. For the most part this was not a problem; funds were used reasonably well. Nevertheless, the grantee NGOs in South Africa didn't expect to be closely monitored and their detailed record-keeping was minimal. Ford, however, brought to its operations a framework for contractual obligations that, in effect, changed the rules of the game. It took awhile for grantee organizations to realize that their Ford program officer was not only substantively involved and interested, but was also keeping an eye on expenditure to see whether the funds were having the intended effect and, if they weren't, to try and fix the problem.

By 1996, when I was given the opportunity to extend my Ford contract for another three years, John Gerhart had found ways to access additional sources of funds in the Ford Foundation beyond a normal budget allocation. These funds enabled me to begin programming on a broader scale while still adhering to the strategy of trying to improve inter-institutional co-ordination in building strategic partnerships between the higher education community and the private sector. The latter strategy was driven by the realization that the ministry of education had much greater needs in public primary and secondary schools than in the relatively well-funded, by African standards, higher education sector.

One strand of grant money sought to bring higher education and the labor market closer together by introducing practices initiated by the Council for Adult and Experiential Learning (CAEL) elsewhere in the world and to address the education and training needs of South Africa's working adults. Working with the Joint Education Trust (JET), Ford supported a variety of CAEL-type activities, but to date, none has really caught on, nor has the effort to strengthen the university and technikon development offices significantly changed the percentage of outside revenues earned by universities and technikons.

Both these initiatives may have been ahead of their time. There is no doubt that the need will grow and, if unmet, will become a burden to the South African economic development agenda. This has been recognized by President Mbeki in his latest state of the nation address.

A related funding strategy was to assist South African universities to become part of a global academic community. Years of sanctions had kept South African academics at home and ignorant of changes underway in the rest of the global education community. Toward this end we supported a three-nation campus diversity project (India, South Africa and the United States) and a three-nation social science curriculum development project (Namibia, Mozambique and South Africa).

At the same time my funding had enough flexibility to focus on special issues, such as the rise of violence against women on campuses, so we funded the creation of a southern African network of projects to reduce that violence. We also funded the establishment of the South African chapter of the Forum for African Women in Education (FAWE), headed by Naledi Pandor, an ANC MP, on the education committee, and Nasima Badsha, the deputy director general for education.

Another special focus was an attempt to introduce the concept of service learning (or community service) to higher education as an activity that was functionally integrated into the curriculum, not just as any old volunteer activity that students did during summer break. This effort also became part of our funding goals with the Association of African Universities, the Working Group in Higher Education and the Association for the Development of Education in Africa (ADEA), a donor group masterfully co-ordinated by Bill Saint of the World Bank for many years.

I needed to be responsive to unanticipated crises and opportunities as well. One such crisis occurred on my birthday in September 1995. I received a call at the Ford Foundation from the late Clive Menell. Clive and his wife, Irene, were close personal friends of Nelson Mandela as well as being the owners of one of South Africa's largest gold mining operations. Clive was calling because Mandela had a problem. In addition to being president of the country, he was also the chancellor of the University of the North, a largely honorific position that he nevertheless took seriously. The students at the University of the North had taken the vice-chancellor hostage and were demanding in effect, ransom to release him. The students did have some legitimate grievances, but paying the ransom, in my judgement, was not the best way forward.

In any case, Clive invited me to a meeting that evening at the president's Houghton residence to discuss the situation. Also present were Irene Menell, Helen Susman and Frederick Van Zyl Slabbert. I called Dorene and told her cryptically that I would be late for my birthday dinner because of a meeting at a "special" house in Houghton. She immediately knew what I meant. I arrived a few minutes early for the meeting. Once past the security guards I made my way to the house where the front door was wide open. I entered and immediately ran into President Mandela; he knew who I was and asked me to help him move some furniture so that our little group could meet comfortably. For the next ten minutes, the world's greatest leader, dressed in bedroom slippers and very casual clothes, and I moved furniture and made small talk. In a sense, the rest of the meeting was anti-climatic. It fell on me to "bell the cat" and to explain to Mandela that what he wanted to do—pay the ransom—was setting a dangerous precedent. After much discussion, we reached a compromise solution: I wrote a grant funded by the Open Society Foundation, represented by Van Zyl Slabbert, which provided funds to the university, but not directly to the student organization, that would address their grievances. The situation was resolved without spreading to other campuses—which had been our great concern.

Another unanticipated demand happened in 1998 when the Ford Foundation's New York-funded Urban Partnership Program decided it wanted to bring approximately two hundred school and community leaders from around the United States to South Africa to experience firsthand what school and community leaders were dealing with during the transition to a post-apartheid South Africa. South Africans didn't really feel ready to share, but the trip went ahead. It was a resounding success and I wrote the Foreword for the book that chronicled the trip and its aftermath:

> I believe that growing up on a farm, as I did, exposes one to the power of experiential learning. Every day and every season one experiences the drama of life and begins to formulate general observations about nature, about people and about the nature of people.
>
> As one reads through the observations and reflections expressed by the participants in the study tour of partnership programs in South Africa by delegates of the American Urban Partnership Program and their South African hosts from the National Centre for Community-Higher Education Partnerships, one is struck by how powerful this experience was in the lives of all who participated. Those of us who have been graced by the opportunity to live in South Africa during the transition from apartheid to a more normal structure of life know that there is something very, very special in the character of South Africans. But even we underestimated the impact this event would have on the thinking and feeling of the participants—American and South Africans alike. South Africans are known for their facility to coin terms to fit situations. Perhaps that reflects what happens when one lives in a multi-

lingual environment. In any case, South Africans who work in the development field coined the derisive term "transformation tourist" to describe the so-called expert—usually from the United States—who jets into Johannesburg, sizes up the situation in two or three days, writes a report telling South Africans how to solve their problems, then visits a game park and flies home. I expected to see a few transformation tourists in the US delegation and frankly it worried me. Consequently, in the planning of this event, I urged the organizers to adapt a structure that I had seen work beautifully with delegates to South Africa from India and the United States in the Ford Foundation's Campus Diversity Initiative a year earlier. The "formula" behind the structure was to immediately immerse all delegates, South Africans and their guests, in a set of site visits and interactions with local people, related to the issues they were going to be discussing. This experience created a common frame of reference to start a meaningful conversation and was followed by an iteration of more site visit experiences and reflective and analytic conversations among delegates. The impact was powerful, constructive and disarming to potential transformation tourists. It was also revealing in that many of the South African delegates had never visited sites selected by the organizers, such as Ghandi's ashram in Durban, or Steve Biko's grave, a situation common to those who have lived all their lives as the victims of apartheid's ugly divisiveness.

They knew of these conditions intellectually, but not experientially, so their learning was fundamentally flawed—a realization brought home rather quickly and which revealed that some South Africans were also guilty of behaving like transformation tourists—making pronouncements on development strategies without ever having really experienced the conditions confronted daily by those they were telling what to do. What the following chapters reveal, once again, is the power of seeing, hearing and experiencing things for the first time. South African and American educators alike were forced to acknowledge that their assumptions and preconceptions about each other and the environments in which partnering for educational advancements is taking place needed re-examination. For the American delegation, the great revelation was how ambitiously the South African partnerships were seeking to deal with profound issues around the development of an equitable, democratic, non-racial society—and by comparison, how meagre their own attempts at home seem. In a powerful way, this trip transformed how they look at themselves. For many in the South African delegation, the opportunity to see themselves, their efforts and their country through the eyes and emotions of their guests was a journey into areas of their own hearts and minds that was new and tremendously reaffirming.

Like so many delegates throughout the week, I was once again moved to tears as I read how this experience affected people, and showed what potential partnerships can have in building lives and communities.

This period was also the start of a deep friendship with Dick Donovan, the director of the Urban Partnership Program, Carolyn Williams, president of Bronx Community College and Barbara Shaier-Peleg, friendships that endure to these last moments.

When I earned some extra pocket money on the farm as a kid, it was a challenge not to allow that money to burn a hole in my pocket, as my grandfather would say, but rather to think long and hard as to how it could best be spent. Thinking long and hard about how one spends one's budget, particularly when the budget comes easily, is one of the greatest challenges a grant maker faces. It's easy to lose sight of the critical, strategic focus and to splash the money around and make a lot of people happy, albeit only for a short time. I think I successfully resisted splashing the money around—although I will acknowledge that not all the grants I made were successful. However, a number of them have had a lasting impact. The funding to CHET is without doubt, the singular most successful investment the Ford Foundation has made in South African higher education. CHET's record of research and publication, of debate and analysis, stands head and shoulders above similar projects undertaken on the African continent over the last decade.

Similarly, the funding that Ford provided on my recommendation to the Artists' Proof Workshop is another example of pushing an organization to a new, sustainable level of operation. It is now able to reach a broad range of young black artists and gradually bring them into a process that provides them with access to formal education and high quality markets. When Dorene and I visited Artists' Proof Workshop's new facilities in 2004, we were humbled by what Kim Berman had done with what, in the grand scope of things, was a modest grant. The Workshop has gained an international reputation; its students have international recognition; and it will continue to provide opportunities for young black artists for years to come.

Neither Kim Berman at Artists' Proof Workshop, nor Nico Cloete at CHET, allowed the extra penny I had given them to burn a hole in their pockets. They thought long and hard about how to invest it and how to make sure it wouldn't be the last penny they received from the Ford Foundation. I think my grandfather would have approved of my efforts.

My work was not exclusively Ford Foundation driven or focused, though undoubtedly it consumed most of my time because it was so enjoyable. Occasionally I was brought on board other activities. One notable example was the effort to create a Fulbright Commission in South Africa. In 1996 the minister of education and the US ambassador appointed a task team to look into the question of whether a formal, joint or bilateral Fulbright Commission between the United States and South Africa should be established. I was appointed to that study group and our findings led us to the recommendation that indeed the time was right and appropriate for such an action. We were proud when the bilateral South African/US Fulbright Commission was created as the fifty-first such commission in the world during the fiftieth anniversary celebration of the creation of the Fulbright Commission. And, I had the honor of being named the founding chair of this commission. In that capacity I had the pleasure of reporting to then vice president Al Gore and deputy president Thabo Mbeki during the occasion of one of their several bi-national commission meetings.

It has always seemed to me that the Fulbright Commission was designed to be an instrument of change and understanding between countries such as the United States and South Africa—countries, that on the one hand claim to have so much in common but, on the other, claim to know so little about each other. I hope the Fulbright

Commission, in whatever form, will continue to provide scholars and researchers from both countries with opportunities for building longer lasting future relationships. For me, working on the SA-US Fulbright Commission was "pay back" for my own Fulbright grant thirty years earlier.

After I retired in 2000, the Ford Foundation made joint grants to CHET and the University of the Witwatersrand that allowed a team of those of us who had been involved in the transformation of South Africa's higher education sector to reflect on these efforts. We commissioned papers, convened workshops and finally published our analyses.

In addition, I was a contributor to the first comprehensive study of private higher education in South Africa; my focus was on the emerging sub-sector of corporate providers of higher education.

My last research effort in South Africa aimed at awakening the country's private-sector leaders to the need for workforce-development policies and programs for managers, supervisors and workers in South Africa's key development industries. My research findings were published in an article in the *Innes Labour Brief*, a leading report for human-resource directors.

The challenges faced by South Africa to catch up with the "global economic express" are many, as are the challenges of keeping the country on its long walk to freedom and democracy.

My efforts to assist these challenges have provided me with a small sense of achievement. I just wish I could stay at the crease for several more innings.

POSTSCRIPT

4:30 p.m. May 3, 2006

Dear Dick [Donovan]

It's been a long, tiring, emotional afternoon.

  I'm so glad Dick has gotten this all down on paper, although I'm sure he could have filled a much larger volume just with South Africa! I have always been aware of how many people and organizations he touched and helped, and in the course of all that never doubted that I, and our family, came before all else. I was never jealous of his involvement or travels. Perhaps it all goes back to the engraving on my wedding rings: "a dream together, of oneness forever". Goodness, I could only say that in an e-mail.

  It's been quite an adventure, precipitated some 48 years ago when he leaned close to me while watching *Around the World in Eighty Days* and whispered, "Marry me and I'll take you around the world." He's always been a man of his word.

Love,
Dorene

[Pressed by time in mid-2005, Dick (Fehnel) asked Dick Donovan to critique the chapter memoirs. A close friendship had developed between the two in the early 1990s with their similar interests and involvement in the Urban Partenrship Program. Upon receipt of a chapter, Dick Donovan would give immediate and honest feedback, and instantly Dick would begin to revise or even call Dick Donovan so they could talk through the suggested edits.]

* * *

Dick was diagnosed in February 2003. One day he was working on the courtyard he'd designed for our home and the next he was recovering from a stent procedure. The doctor commented, "Oh, by the way, the chest x-ray shows a minute spot on your left lung." I think we both knew we were in an unwinnable battle but we were both determined to do everything possible to seek the most effective treatment while continuing to live life to the fullest, for as long as we could.

The memoirs weren't started until early summer 2005 and Dick's plan was to surprise me at his birthday gathering on September 26, and read the first chapter. Thankfully I stumbled onto his endeavor, otherwise I wouldn't have held up, emotionally, through the reading. Dick's writing progress slowed somewhat as he continued to work on education-related projects, the holidays approached and we were planning a trip to Spain in February 2006. He was determined we'd go on that trip with our dear friends and trusted travel companions, Rosemary and Walt Ellis. The prospect saw him through his last round of chemo. Not long after our return in March, and as the oncologist had predicted, he suddenly hit the wall and was hospitalized late in April.

So here was the mother of all deadlines, as I can hear Dick saying. I'm sure there were those who thought finishing the memoirs was inconsequential and I briefly asked myself "Why am I encouraging this when I should be sitting beside him 24/7?" Walt was sent out to purchase two tape recorders, one to put beside his bed and the other sitting beside me at the computer. Once it was determined he wouldn't be coming home because of his oxygen needs and was moved to Hopewell House Hospice, Dick fielded phone calls, interspersed visits with friends and family, while jotting down his thoughts on a pad. When he was done he would dictate a section. As determined and focused as he appeared, he did not want me to leave his side. We resolved this by asking Rosemary to come over for a few hours each morning to read Alexander McCall Smith's book *Blue Shoes and Happiness* to him. It worked beautifully, allowing me to go home and type like I've never typed before knowing only I could transcribe his words. I recall someone suggesting I hire a typist, but the sound was difficult because of his 30% oxygen need and only I knew the names, places, incidents he was relating. And, Rosemary's reading transported him, albeit briefly, back to a part of the world he loved so dearly.

The last dictation was done on Wednesday, May 3. Dick began to sleep more. On Saturday a copy was printed out and during one of his wakeful moments I showed it to him. Just a little before 11 p.m. that night he quietly slipped away and as I left Hopewell House with our son, granddaughter, Rosemary and Walt, a gentle Oregon rain was falling.

Dorene Fehnel
September 2007

BIBLIOGRAPHY

Alda, Alan. *Never Have Your Dog Stuffed and Other Things I've Learned.* Random House. 2005.
Bradley, James & Powers, Ron. *Flags of Our Fathers.* Bantam, 2006.
Brokaw, Tom. *A Long Way from Home: Growing Up in the American Heartland in the Forties and Fifties.* Random House. 2002.
Cloete, Nico; Fehnel, Richard; Maassen, Peter; Moja, Teboho; Perold, Helene; Gibbon, Trish. *Transformation in Higher Education: Global Pressures and Local Realities in South Africa.* Juta. 2002.
Clegg, Johnny & Savuka. "Your Time Will Come". *Heat, Dust and Dreams.* EMI Records. 1993.
Doig, Ivan. *The House of Sky: Landscapes of a Western Mind.* Harvest. 1980.
Donovan, Richard A. & Wolfe, Lois (eds). *South African Journeys.* National Center of Educational Alliances. 1998.
Fehnel, R. & Sundberg, N. *From Apathy to Awareness, Action and Assimilation: A Model for Institutional Development of Experiential Learning in a Traditional University.* The Office of Institutional Research, California State Universities and College. 1978.
Frey, James. *A Million Little Pieces.* Anchor. 2003.

Groopman, Jerome. *The Anatomy of Hope: How People Prevail in the Face of Illness*. Random House. 2004.

Guba, Evon; Lincoln, G; Yvonna, S. *Fourth Generation Evaluation*. Sage. 1989.

Horowitz, Irving Louis (ed.). *The Rise and Fall of Project Camelot: Studies in the Relationship Between Social Science and Practical Politics*. MIT Press. 1967.

Hunt, Linda Lawrence. *Bold Spirit: Helga Estby's Forgotten Walk Across Victorian America*. Anchor. 2003.

Kerrigan, Lynn. *Scrapple: The Pennsylvania Treat*. Accessed 2006. www.globalgourmet.com/food/sleuth/0998/phili.html.

Kruss, Glenda & Kraak, Andre. *A Contested Good? Private Higher Education in South Africa*. Boston College Center for International Higher Education. 2003.

Lehrer, Jim. *A Bus of My Own*. Putnam. 1992.

Pirsig, Robert M. *Zen and the Art of Motorcycle Maintenance*. HarperTorch. 2006.

Russert, Tim. *Big Russ and Me. Father and Son: Lessons of Life*. Miramax. 2006.

Wolpe, AnnMarie. *The Long Way Home*. Virago. 1994.

www.ingramcontent.com/pod-product-compliance
Lightning Source LLC
Chambersburg PA
CBHW011139290426
44108CB00020B/2691